# new life

## FOR OLD GARDENS

# ALLAN SEALE

*Illustrations by Lorrie Lawrence*

NEW
HOLLAND

# The Lady Who Was Here Before

There are some people that I hate,
They gather at my garden gate,
Discussing, till I'm sick and sore,
The Lady Who Was Here Before.
They stand and whisper: 'What a shame.
I'm thankful Mrs What's-her-name
is dead, poor dear, and doesn't know.
She used to love her garden so.
'They've thrown away those lovely rocks
She got from Cheddar—and the Box
She planted round her heart-shaped plots
of Heartsease and Forget-me-nots.
'They've moved her Salpiglossis bed,
And planted Primulas instead.
They've put an ugly Poplar tree
Where that nice Privet used to be.'
They'll get me so upset, some day.
That I shall spring at them, and say:
This is my garden. GO AWAY!

Reginald Arkell

This edition published in 2002 by
New Holland Publishers (UK) Ltd

First published in Australia in 1999 by
New Holland Publishers (Australia) Pty Ltd
Sydney • Auckland • London • Cape Town
www.newhollandpublishers.com

Level 1, Unit 4, 14 Aquatic Drive, Frenchs Forest, NSW 2086, Australia
218, Lake Road, Northcote, Auckland, New Zealand
Garfield House, 86-88 Edgware Road, London W2 2EA, United Kingdom
80 McKenzie Street, Cape Town 8001, South Africa

Publishing General Manager: Jane Hazell
Publisher: Averill Chase
Commissioning Editor: Derelie Evely
Project Editor: Monica Ban
Project Consultant: Judy Moore
Designer: Kerry Klinner
Artwork: Lorrie Lawrence
Reproduction: Colour Symphony
Printer: Tien Wah Press

ISBN 1 84330 312 4

Every reasonable effort has been made to contact copyright holders of
'The Lady Who Was Here Before' by Reginald Arkell. The publisher would
be pleased to hear from copyright holders to rectify any errors or omissions.

Page 2: Striking pink rhododendrons and soft lilac wisteria will complement any colourful courtyard setting.
Page 6: New to the area, the owners decided to give their garden a complete makeover. The gently sloping garden
was levelled to provide a series of 'rooms'. A parterre garden, with its central armillary sphere sundial is shown under
construction and in its sun-drenched completion a season or two later.

# contents

# prelude

This book is designed to meet the needs of people with a garden that has outgrown its youthful exuberance. Dominant plantings are demanding more than the anticipated share of root space, and maturing trees are now providing shady canopies over sun-loving plants.

Whether you've recently purchased an older house and are bewildered by an overgrown garden or are re-evaluating your own established landscape, you'll find suggestions for easy rejuvenations that will renew the garden with minimal effort.

Here is a practical guide to help you evaluate the site, soil and existing greenery as well as hints on pruning, transplanting and rejuvenating lawns, paths and walls together with plantings to give you many years of pleasurable, easy-care gardening.

*Allan Seale*

# *appraising*

## YOUR GARDEN

# CHANGING CHARACTER OF GARDENS

As gardens mature, subtle changes occur. Trees grow and throw shade on areas once bathed in full sun, a gardener's interest veers off in another direction requiring space for a hobby collection, or maybe a larger outdoor area is needed for entertaining.

RIGHT: *Subtle blending of colours combining flowers, foliage, urn and shell grit on the driveway provide foreground interest as elements graduate in height to established, taller-growing shrubs at the rear.*

OPPOSITE: *A sheltered courtyard with a maturing Japanese maple casting shade over an increasingly patchy lawn. This has been given an enticing makeover using paving, a pond with giant-sized stepping stones and colour co-ordinated shade-loving spring flowering plants. Seasonal potted colour can be changed to golden tones to complement the autumn colouring of the maple leaves as they begin to fall.*

A well-cared-for garden, even one that is well loved, can gradually lose individuality as shrubs grow and spread beyond their allotted space, becoming a shapeless mass as they try to out-jostle each other. The more dominant plants grab more than their share of sunlight, soil moisture and nutrients, causing the less vigorous ones, that once added so much variety and interest to the garden, to become twiggy and starved-looking — if they are to survive at all.

For the same reason, much of the lawn may look like a worn carpet, having a similar effect on the appearance of the overall landscape as a threadbare carpet would have on a room.

In some cases this gradual deterioration creeps up on its owners unnoticed. Some accept it as inevitable while others seem to be forever fighting a frustrating battle, trying to grow the same type and quality of flowers or grass that they once enjoyed.

The only answer is to accept that as time moves on, gardens grow and therefore must change. Don't fight this change, rather embrace it. Without great effort or expense, the garden can be revived, while you gain more enjoyment from it, with less work.

Drastic and expensive landscaping schemes are not suggested. Small improvements or additions made gradually can soon bring interest and charm back into the garden.

# FACELIFTS FOR TIRED GARDENS

**W**hen taking over a house with a neglected garden, many see its surroundings only as a bewildering tangle of plant growth. Too often their reaction is to clear away the lot and to start again from scratch.

OPPOSITE: *Concrete paving slabs set in a slight curve replace a previously laid double-breasted slab path with minimal planting. Dead wood, old leaves and cobwebs were removed while creepers and shrubs were under-pruned to allow low-growing plants to thrive under their canopy. The slabs have been laid in a single line to give visual width and to accommodate the plants tumbling over them.*

 A great many old or neglected gardens are hiding numerous specimens that in their untidy state may look ugly and past their prime to all but the expert gardener's eye. However, with a little attention many of these 'ugly ducklings' could be transformed in just one season to become delightful eye-catchers! Also appreciate that the old garden may still contain a wealth of now-dormant bulbs and herbaceous perennials.

Even once popular overgrown shrubs like cotoneasters, weigelas, abelias, taller-type azaleas and camellias can be transformed into either compact domes, graceful espaliers to hide old fences or, in some cases, the taller-growing species can have lower branches removed so that they become small shade trees, changing their character and opening up pleasant vistas through the garden (see Pruning Trees and Shrubs p 60).

Irrespective of the value other people attach to its original plantings and style, the garden should be as you like it and contain what you like. It would certainly be monotonous if all gardens conformed to a set formula.

However, it is wise to live with your initial plans for a time because familiarity with your garden and those in the neighbourhood sometimes modifies ideas. Better to aim for something that looks comfortably relaxing and complementary. The spectacular can become tiresome.

It often helps to look at other gardens, also to see what some of the original plantings could look like after rejuvenation. Don't assess their worth in winter when some are at their lowest ebb. Consider moving any in doubt to a more suitable position but don't bear with them if you can't agree with other people's assessment.

If the garden is heavily shaded and dark, consider lifting the canopy of the overhead branches to allow more light in under the trees and plant the area with light-green-coloured plants such as the soft shield fern (*Polystichum setiferum*). Other ruses the gardener can use to lift dark areas is to make use of white flowers and variegated foliage. There are a number of hardy plants to use, such as the strappy leafed *Lirope muscari* 'Variegata' and *Ligularia dentata* with its large spotted leaves.

Remember that local councils may refuse permission for removal of trees with a girth more than 12 cm (5 in) in diameter unless dangerously close to buildings. If neighbours are critical about the removal of a shrub, why not offer that they may have it if they care to dig it out, or offer them cuttings. Remember that it is now your garden and should be as you like it.

# TACKLING THE TASK OF RENEWAL

*T*ake time to assess both the positive and negative points of an overgrown garden. An untidy shrub may only require a vigorous prune, and what appears to be a dead shrub in winter may well delight you with spring blossoms or fabulous autumn colours.

OPPOSITE: *The silvery trunk of a mature eucalypt stands out in sharp relief to the newer group planting under its high canopy.*

BELOW: *Potted colour can be the answer where an actual garden is not possible.*

On investigation, a mound of growth may be covering up a beautiful rock ledge which could change your entire concept of how you want the garden to look.

Stand back, take a good objective look at the garden and try to assess its worst feature. If this does not stand out, choose a part that looks dreary, or a section that you would prefer not to include in a photograph. It often helps to view the garden from a window — to 'frame' a picture — in effect, providing a focal or starting point in a design of a particular section.

Sometimes in making decisions on what to keep and what to discard, it helps to have the opinion of someone who has not seen the garden for some time. However, here the drawback can be that they are too polite to criticise, or their tastes may differ from yours. If you have been patronising the local nursery and built up a rapport with staff over the years, you may care to ask for an appraisal of the garden. This will of course be at a cost, but a horticulturalist with local plant and climate knowledge does provide an unbiased opinion. You may know what you want your garden to look like but are not sure how to go about it — begin by collecting pictures in books such as this to show to the consultant when an on-site visit is planned.

Don't feel that you have to rush out and begin the garden renewal the week you move in — rather, enjoy this period of observation and decision-making. The actual digging, pruning and installation of new projects are usually a continuing evolvement in the life of a garden and a family, and even your 'must do' initial ideas may change as you appreciate the subtleties which occur with the changing seasons.

# WHAT TYPE OF GARDEN?

Y ou may find that when an existing garden is cleared up a little and old shrubbery rejuvenated or replaced, the general effect is pleasant and satisfying. The question then is — where to from here? The choice of garden styles is wide.

 Where trees predominate, why not a woodland garden? This can become attractive with very little maintenance, and falling leaves, a natural cycle, become future compost.

If after the clean-up there is very little worth salvaging, look at replanning possibilities. For example, if the garden has rectangular spaces where lawns have been, straight or angular paths, steps or terracing, it is easily converted to the formal style garden popular in the late 19th or early 20th century and now enjoying a fashionable comeback.

Should the cleaned-up area be fairly open, then a wild-flower garden with predominately native plants is yet another possibility. This is fairly quick to establish but appreciate the fact that many of the quicker-growing wild plants are comparatively short-lived and may need periodic replacement.

A Japanese garden can also be attractive, easy to maintain, and need not strictly conform to the traditional concept. Capturing its typical serene and restful atmosphere requires mainly a good sense of symmetry, balance and restraint when planning plantings and features.

Gardens with large shade areas adapt well to Japanese gardens. Elements of the garden can be kept simple, such as a few well-placed stepping stones encouraged to become mossy, dwarf compact shrubs or clipped azaleas, perhaps a stone lantern and a few shade-tolerant uprights such as nandina, fatsia and clump-forming bamboo species. The latter can be safely contained for years in low tubs.

Probably the easiest garden adaptable to any site, old or new, is one most popular today, not following any particular tradition and perhaps incorporating trends from all types, including the recently revived cottage garden theme.

Let's call this the 'Free Form' garden because geometrical components like boundaries are planted out or at least softened by plantings. Borders between lawns and plant beds flow in graceful curves.

Except for occasional contrast, most trees or shrubs, even though pruned, are allowed to retain their natural form. This type of garden is perhaps the best choice when rejuvenating old gardens, because areas where lawns no longer grow well can easily be incorporated into adjoining beds of more adaptable plants, by reducing or changing a curve or the same treatment used to extend the lawn.

Sweeping curves usually make a garden look more spacious by lengthening the perimeter of borders and/or allowing some sections of the

# Adding Enjoyment to Outdoor Living

**Key**

1. Vegetable garden.
2. Chinese star jasmine (*Trachelospermum jasminoides*)
3. *Escallonia macrantha* 'Apple Blossom'.
4. Arch with Rosa 'Clair Matin'.
5. Crape myrtle (*Lagerstroemia indica*).
6. *Paulownia fortunei*
7. Transplanted red bush roses
8. Mock orange (*Philadelphus coronarius*)

lawn to disappear around a clump of shrubbery or low-branching tree. The latter trick also adds interest by causing speculation about the hidden sections of the garden.

## Other points to consider

• Barbeque or other outdoor living areas, which for preference should be handy to the kitchen and have some privacy.

• Paving is preferable to lawn around these areas because grass wears where foot traffic is concentrated. The outdoor living area would obviously be incorporated with a swimming pool if one is present or planned. In the latter case, consider access for excavation and building equipment, and also pool fencing.

• Children's play area — preferably, this should adjoin outdoor living amenities, be in good view of the kitchen and, if possible, living room areas.

ABOVE: *The traditional layout of a back garden has been cleverly transformed, by the addition of curved beds, into passive and active sections. The clothes line is hidden from view behind a hedge.*

# CREATING VISTAS

Vistas add tremendous interest to a garden just as a pleasant view will enhance it and add a sense of generous proportion. If you are fortunate enough to have a scenic view from any portion of the garden, plan to feature it.

 This need not mean automatically removing obstructing trees or shrubbery. It can look far more interesting if framed, just as a landscape painting or photograph gains when framed by a tree or branch on at least one side. In other words, all you may have to do is trim off some lower or side branches or perhaps plant a high-branching tree in a position where it will do the framing.

Alternatively, you can create a more interesting picture if a distant vista, a beautiful tree or a planting is viewed through a pergola, arch or gateway.

One of the landscaping laws frequently offered is to plant out along the boundaries of a garden. However, greater interest and illusion of size, even in a small garden, can be achieved by leaving a break here and there, although it may initially expose the often-maligned paling fence. From most viewing points, this can increase the area by several metres (feet), depending on the width of the shrubbery on either side, perhaps more according to the way you treat it, as well as creating interest.

A section of fence can become the focal point if masked with lattice or brushwood, or painted green and partly covered by perhaps a climbing rose if in a sunny spot, a creeper that does not project from it or, say, an espaliered camellia.

The main thing to avoid is striking colour that will jump out at you. This will wreck the impression of greater distance. Close to the fence may be a good place for a seat. This usually adds interest and a relaxed feeling to the garden; it could also be a warm sheltered spot on cold days. You could build a pergola over it for shade. Cover it with a deciduous vine like ornamental grape that lets plenty of sun through in winter, gives cool shade during summer and then a grand finale of colour in autumn.

In the case of a seat, whether under a pergola or not, some form of solid paving would be appropriate. You may prefer a combination of paving where practical and some form of easy-care ground cover.

## ILLUSIONS AND OTHER TRICKS

The illusion of distance can be created by diminishing the size of objects the further they are away from a viewing point.

For example, where a window is looking on to a fence or wall a short distance away, you might favour a Japanese scene. Give it distance by placing a small to medium-size stone lantern in the foreground and another smaller one further away, perhaps on the edge of one of those easily constructed fibreglass pools. Let the scene taper away and disappear behind a small clumpy shrub or a mound which becomes a small hill. Stepping stones winding between the stone lanterns and over the distant hill, starting off large and getting smaller in size as they disappear over the hill or in behind the shrub hiding the end of the pond, will add to the illusion.

Another trick that gardeners can use to deceive the eye is trompe l'oeil designs painted on a masonry wall. This artistic approach provides an illusion of distance and is invaluable where space is tight. However, if you are not too good with the paintbrush, yet hanker after the feeling of virtual space, ready-made trompe l'oeil lattice arch designs are available which can be easily attached to a wall. Place a potted plant on either side of the arch and the illusion is complete.

Landscape painters can teach us fabulous lessons about colour, shape and texture. They work on an entirely flat surface yet they create the impression of distance. Notice that they achieve this by keeping their brighter greens, bluer water, etc, in the foreground, then fade these away as distance increases. Close hills are probably greens with browns, becoming blue as they recede, then fade to soft blue-grey or pale mauve or grey.

*BELOW: Generous, sweeping garden beds accentuate the line of the hills behind, which the owners of this country garden have not obscured by thoughtfully selecting relatively low-growing plants.*

**Key**

1. Swane's golden cypress (*Cupressus sempervirens* 'Swane's Golden')
2. Box (*Buxus sempervirens* 'Suffruticosa')
3. *Rosa* 'Crepescule'
4. Wisteria (*Wisteria sinensis*)
5. *Rosa* 'Black Boy'
6. Crab apple (*Malus floribunda*)
7. Camellia (*Camellia* x *williamsii* 'Waterlily')
8. *Rosa* 'Mrs Anthony Waterer'
9. Dogwood (*Cornus florida*)

## CREATING VISTAS WITH PLANTS AND PERGOLA

*L*ate spring and the outdoors beckon. As well as providing a sheltered spot pergolas can be used to create an illusionary perspective of space in even the smallest of gardens. Note how the use of a focal point at the end of a short path draws the eye through and beyond the pergola. Likewise the opening between the clipped box hedge invites the eye across the lawn to the perennial border.

# THE POWER OF COLOUR, TEXTURE AND FORM

G ardens are composed of separate plants. How we combine them with all the design elements is what creates an individual and pleasing style.

OPPOSITE: A series of flowing curves leads the eye to a number of focal points within this well-ordered garden. The immediate impact of the bold colours in the foreground is repeated to a lesser extent in the garden beyond the pergola, while the racemes of wisteria blossom accentuate the dripping fountain and the weeping golden foliage of the conifer Cupressus macrocarpa 'Aurea Saligna' beyond.

The idea of breaking the usual line of boundary-masking shrubbery can be extended by combining shrubs into groups of complementary shapes and colours. Achieving this grouped effect may mean eliminating one or two shrubs here and there that no longer contribute attractively to the general effect, or perhaps moving them to a more suitable position.

Apart from providing much more scope for variety and interest between the groups of shrubbery, the combination of forms adds another dimension. For example, you may group two or three different-sized dome-shaped shrubs with a tallish conical form, with the largest partly behind and the others placed unevenly either side in the foreground. The next group may be a placement of four or five dome shapes of varying sizes, perhaps with a low-spreading type towards the foreground or sides, or a combination of fan-shaped and rounded or conical types. Combinations are endless, especially if the gardener is prepared to regularly clip plants into shape.

Fences bared by breaking the shrub line can be covered with well-behaved climbing plants (see list p 98). What you have gained in space can then be used to grow roses (if a sunny spot),

flowering perennials or seasonal annuals. If you lack time or the inclination for this, just cover the area with easy care but attractive ground cover plants listed on page 88.

If you want to minimise plantings, you will still retain interest from the grouping idea, and a feeling of greater space can be achieved by swinging the lawn in to take up some of the area.

## COLOUR

There are many small colourful foliage plants as well as flowering shrubs that can keep the garden bright and cheerful throughout the seasons. At the same time, don't forget the many delightful shades of green.

There are gardens where the atmosphere is so relaxing, almost serene, because greens predominate without the distraction of strong colours. The important thing is to choose what

### COLOUR PLANTING

Colourful planting can be used to give the impression of extra depth to the garden. Use brighter colours in the foreground and softer ones towards the boundary.

pleases you most — think how monotonous it would be if gardens were all the same!

Colours need not be bright to catch the eye. Even white can become a feature in combination with green or a muted colour. Effective colour schemes that come to mind are a gracefully weeping white or soft cream broom (*Cytisus* x *praecox*) in front of a dark bronze Japanese maple, backed by a dark laurel hedge from a neighbouring garden. Also a clump of ice-blue to white tall bearded iris in front of dark yew, silver-grey *Senecio cineraria* 'Silver Dust' with bronze foliaged *Berberis thunbergii* and a white double-flowered form of May (*Spiraea cantoniensis*) cascading on to a green lawn.

Blue, like grey, has a softening and distancing effect, but complements every bright colour as well as the softer more muted ones. It springs to life with white, cream and bronze. Another of the many delightful colour combinations I recall is a large, deep-blue dome of ceanothus against a crisp white double spring-flowering peach; also perennial blue salvia intermingled with 'Iceberg' roses. Lavender gives a similar although slightly softer effect than these.

Again, the combinations are almost endless, as they are with the brighter primary-coloured flowers of the fashionable cannas and dahlias, and yellow and white variegated foliage plants such as aucuba and the decorative grasses.

## STYLE WITH SILVER AND GREY

Silver- and grey-foliage plants have long been associated with adding a stylish finishing touch to sunny gardens.

Grey-foliaged plants are often used as backgrounds to give the impression of greater distance. At the same time, they conveniently provide a wonderful foil and complement all the brighter colours, especially gold and reds. These include all the bluish-grey lavenders, silvery-grey wormwood, the soft lacy dusty millers and, on a slightly smaller scale, cotton lavender, Aurora daisy and others.

On a larger scale for temperate gardens, there are some varieties of Australian silver-grey wattle and the coastal tea-tree (*Leptospermum scoparium* 'Keatleyi'). On a taller scale, several eucalypts can give the effect of misty distance. There is a wide choice of both dwarf and tall conifers; also, the pendulous grey or willow-leafed *Pyrus salicifolia* 'Glauca' and others. The quick-growing variegated box elder (*Acer negundo* 'Variegatum'), with its dull green and white foliage combination, can create a massive pyramid of distant-looking foliage. Deciduous, yes, but the leafless branches are softened by flimsy cascades of seed catkins.

BELOW: *Winter colour is an important ingredient to aim for especially in cold climates where many trees and shrubs are bare. Here, atop a dry pack wall, a perennial wallflower* Erysimum *'Bowles Mauve' provides vivid proof of the power of colour, while a rosemary bush below provides the other wonderful garden ingredients — silver foliage and scent.*

# Low-growing Silver-grey Foliaged Perennials

Many of these plants, while growing to a height of 50 cm (1½ ft) or more, have a spreading habit.
All prefer full sun or at least half-sun.

| Common name | Botanical name | Details |
| --- | --- | --- |
| | *Achillea nana* | strongly aromatic foliage, white flowers in summer |
| Aurora daisy | *Arctotis hybrida* | long-flowering during the hotter summer months; tends to be grown as an annual |
| Cardoon | *Cynara cardunculus* | magnificent background statement often reaching 2 m (6 ft) in height. |
| Catmint | *Nepeta* x *faassenii* | creates a soft blue-grey carpet |
| Cotton lavender | *Santolina chamaecyparissus* | narrow, slender leaves topped with yellow flowers in summer |
| Dusty miller | *Senecio cineraria* 'Silver Dust' | Interesting silver-grey serrated foliage; small yellow flowers in summer, which are best removed |
| | *Eryngium variifolium* | thistle-like grey-blue flowers in late summer |
| Globe artichoke | *Cynara scolymus* | wonderful accent plant and edible flower buds! |
| | *Helichrysum petiolare* | give it ample space as it can spread up to 1.5 m (5 ft) |
| Iris | *Iris*, Bearded Hybrids | all bearded types are hardy and rewarding |
| Lavender | *Lavandula angustifolia* and *L. dentata* | use singly or in groups |
| Lamb's tongue | *Stachys byzantina* | ground-hugging plants with soft felty leaves |
| Pinks | *Dianthus* species | spring-flowering carpeter |
| | *Primula auricula* | Soft, grey-green leaves are densely covered with white farina |
| Rock cress | *Arabis caucasica* | white spring flowers, can be used to overplant spring bulbs |
| Rosemary | *Rosmarinus officinalis* | culinary herb at home in the flower garden |
| Sea campion | *Silene uniflora* | carpeting perennial with white summer blooms |
| Silverlace | *Tanacetum haradjanii* | Interesting silver-grey serrated foliage and bright yellow summer flowers |
| Snow-in-summer | *Cerastium tomentosum* | a carpeting plant with white summer flowers |
| Society garlic | *Tulbaghia violacea* | clump-forming with narrow leaves and lilac flowers |
| Succulents | many species | hardy plants with interesting foliage |
| Wormwood | *Artemisia absinthium* *A. arborescens,* *A. caucasica, A. ludoviciana* | all these plants have silvery decorative foliage |
| Yarrow | *Achillea* 'Moonshine' | feathery grey-green leaves with yellow flowers in summer |

# Silver-grey Foliaged Shrubs and Trees

This list includes grey-leafed shrubs or trees to add style to any garden, no matter what size.

| Common name | Botanical name | Details |
|---|---|---|
| Arizona cypress | *Cupressus arizonica* | makes an excellent specimen tree |
| Conifers | *Cedrus atlantica* 'Glauca'<br>*Picea glauca* 'Coerulea'<br>*Abies concolor* 'Argentea' | an excellent cool-climate specimen tree; also called 'Atlas cedar'.<br>needle-like, blue-green to silver leaves.<br>silvery foliage contrasts well with dark grey bark |
| | *Brachyglottyis* 'Sunshine' | yellow daisy-like flowers cover interesting foliage in summer |
| | *Buddleia* 'Lochinch' | lilac-coloured blooms are sweetly perfumed |
| Creeping Juniper | *Juniperus horizontalis* | wide-spreading, mat-forming shrub |
| Eucalypts<br>  Mountain gum<br>  Snow gum<br>  Tingiringi gum | *Eucalyptus dalrympleana*<br>*E. pauciflora*<br>*E. glaucescens* | white flowers in late summer.<br>red-rimmed, grey-green leaves.<br>leaves are silvery-blue when young, blue-grey when mature |
| Germander | *Teucrium fruticans* | slender-leafed shrub often used for hedging |
| Jerusalem sage | *Phlomis fruticosa* | whorls of golden-yellow flowers produced amid sage-like, grey-green foliage |
| Oleaster | *Elaeagnus angustifolia* | bushy shrub, silvery-grey leaves, fragrant creamy-yellow flowers |
| | *Potentilla fruticosa* 'Manchu' | pure white flowers borne amid divided silvery-grey leaves |
| | *Ruta graveolens* 'Jackman's Blue' | aromatic, blue-grey foliage, mustard-yellow flowers in summer |
| Sawara false cypress<br>  cultivars | *Chamaecyparis pisifera* 'Nana'<br>*C.p.* 'Squarrosa Intermedia' and<br>*C.p.* 'Boulevard' | knee-high carpeter;<br>these varieties give added form, texture and colour interest |
| Tea-tree | *Leptospermum scoparium*<br>'Keatleyi' | aromatic grey-green leaves with pink flowers in summer |
| Veronica | *Hebe albicans*<br>*Hebe* 'E.A. Bowles'<br>*Hebe recurva* | distinctive foliage with greyish blooms in summer<br>produces slender spikes of lilac flowers through to late autumn<br>blue-grey leaves, white flowers in summer |
| Woody willow | *Salix lanata* | bushy dense shrub with wooly grey shoots and silver-grey leaves |
| Wattle<br>  Cootamundra wattle<br><br>  Queensland silver wattle<br>  Ovens wattle | *Acacia baileyana*<br><br>*A. podalyriifolia*<br>*A. pravissima* | with masses of ball-shaped flowers in late winter–early spring; better in warmer positions<br>with golden ball-shaped flowers in late winter<br>silver-grey phyllodes, small yellow flowers in late winter–early spring |

# THE IMPORTANCE OF CLIMATE AND SOIL

*When moving to an unfamiliar area, you will be rewarded when you take into account the two main influences on a garden.*

Gardeners can appreciate that there are considerable climatic differences between, say, north and south, but sometimes fail to realise that even within the same city there can be tremendous changes in both climate and soil type. These two factors have an important bearing on what plants will thrive in your garden.

Climate can be defined for gardeners as temperature and rainfall and, to a lesser extent, wind. It is the extremes of temperature that must be taken into consideration when dealing with plant choice as many plants will survive, but not thrive, when temperatures are not to their liking.

Many exotic plants used in horticulture are sourced from areas experiencing a regular rainfall pattern, while many Australian plants, for instance, have adapted to a dry environment and can exist with limited rainfall. Alternatively, they can be planted in raised garden beds.

Luckily we can create a microclimate to accommodate favourite plants by making use of any natural features which help to change the general climatic pattern. For example, a southern aspect and slope of a garden can increase the range of heat-loving plants. Equally, if the garden lacks these natural advantages then extra warmth can be had by planting against a south-facing wall or providing shelter such as a greenhouse. Plants that are frost-tender can often be accommodated under an overhanging tree or eave, while planting shrubs to reduce pollution or act as a filter against salt-laden wind allows a greater diversity of plants to be grown within a garden. However, except perhaps for an occasional special, most plants stocked by a reliable local nursery are there because they suit the district.

Also, when moving to a new area, appreciate that your new soil may be different to that of the garden you have left. Fortunately, the majority of plants adapt to most soil types. Don't be too downhearted if close neighbours tell you that the soils in your area are very poor.

This accusation applies more often to loams that contain an appreciable amount of clay — they are sticky when wet, and set hard and are unyielding when dry. These soils can be made productive if dug, planted or disturbed in any way when they reach a damp stage, then mulched with compost or similar fibrous material to protect them from the puddling effect of heavy rain or watering.

Quick-drying sandy soil is also gradually improved by the addition of compost lightly worked in, and as a surface mulch.

# identifying

## AND SOLVING

## PROBLEMS

# REVITALISING A LACKLUSTRE GARDEN

*O*nce the initial hurly-burly of moving house has settled, there is time to examine the garden in detail. Often it is hard to pinpoint any particular trouble spot even though the garden certainly looks in need of an overall revitalising design program.

An uninteresting garden could result from shrubs that are now growing in together and therefore have lost their individual character, or plants such as tall azaleas showing too much bare or twiggy lower growth.

In either case the answer is pruning. Try to bring individual shrubs back to original form and vary their heights. You can go further and add some character to the garden by removing one or two of the least attractive shrubs here and there to bring the others into interesting groups of different forms (see The Power of Colour, Texture and Form on p 22).

It can also be a case of less is more, so consider leaving air space around some fine old specimens so that after re-shaping and pruning

## Within a Season

**1.** When a keen gardener moved in, straight beds were given a gentle curve, and hard clay soil was made workable with the addition of organic material and gypsum.

**2.** The lawn was revitalised, beds planted with a plethora of favourite plants and, within a season or two, the fence was well-hidden from view by a wall of colour.

# Taming an Unkempt Garden

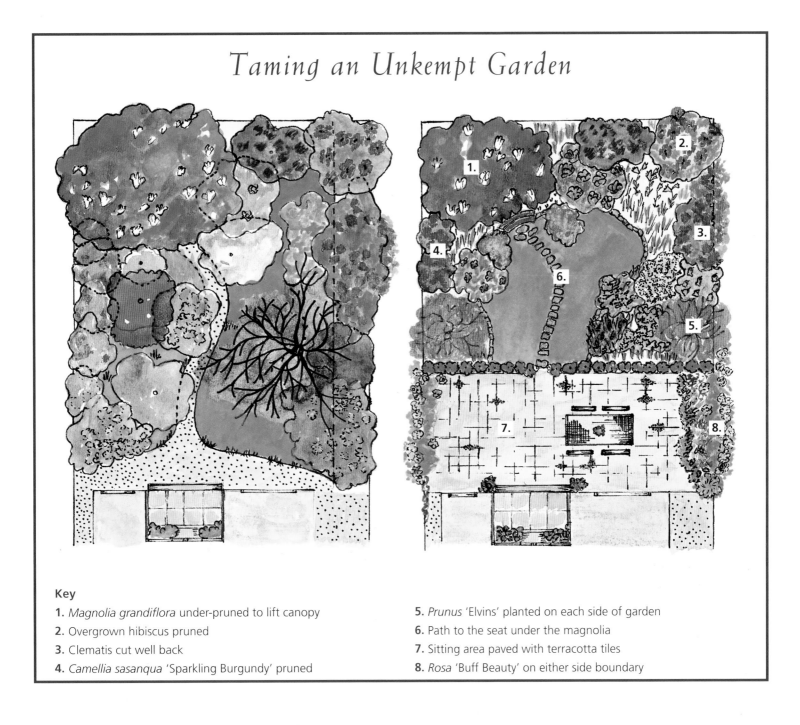

**Key**

1. *Magnolia grandiflora* under-pruned to lift canopy
2. Overgrown hibiscus pruned
3. Clematis cut well back
4. *Camellia sasanqua* 'Sparkling Burgundy' pruned
5. *Prunus* 'Elvins' planted on each side of garden
6. Path to the seat under the magnolia
7. Sitting area paved with terracotta tiles
8. *Rosa* 'Buff Beauty' on either side boundary

they again have a chance to flourish. These spaces can be used for interesting but low-growing easy-care plantings and also give the garden more generous-looking proportions. If adding other plants to complete these shrub groups, or between them, note particularly the following chapter Why New Plants Fail, p 42, which deals with how to incorporate new plantings into established groups where they have to compete for root space.

*ABOVE: The need for an outdoor living area within an overgrown garden has been resolved by dividing the garden in two with a low box hedge.*

# SHADE, WHERE ONCE WAS SUN

The most common cause of dissatisfaction with a mature garden is shade. We welcome it in summer but overhanging tree canopies and greedy roots can inhibit the growth of many colourful plants, making a re-think essential to pleasurable gardening.

*OPPOSITE: The colour green, especially that of the lighter tones of most ferns, is a wonderful foil for deep-shaded areas whether caused by dense overhead foliage or nearby buildings. The tree ferns with large spreading fronds and slender tall trunks can be grouped with those of a slower-growing habit on short stout trunks to form a multi-tiered glade or they can be combined with many of the ground-hugging species plus a pond or birdbath to add to the serene atmosphere.*

Is the problem a shady, rather desolate-looking area situated below overhanging large shrubbery, or trees where the lawn no longer grows? Then consider these possibilities:

- The simplest is to extend the line of the garden or shrub bed out to encompass the area of poor growth. If the shade is not too dense and the soil surface is not matted with surface roots, azaleas should suit. Plant them with the top of their root ball a centimetre or two above the soil surface, building up to this with a little fairly well-rotted lime-free compost, then mulch with a layer of compost or woodchip. This will help them to make their shallow root-mat above existing roots.

- If shade is dense or the position is north-facing, try establishing a group of 'Mrs Robb's Bonnet' (*Euphorbia amygloidies* var. *robbiae*). This evergreen spurge is apt to be invasive in 'ideal' situations, but here will be kept in check by the root competition and the lack of light. The rosettes of shiny, dark green leaves make good ground cover and the greenish-yellow cymes of flowers carried in the spring bring a welcome splash of colour into the dark, moody shade. *Vinca minor*, the lesser periwinkle, grown in and around the spurge, will add further colour and interest to the area, with its small purple, blue or white flowers in spring and early summer.

- If part or full sun streams in under the tree of shrub canopy, why not try agapanthus? They are root-tolerant, but do need some sun to flower well. Their high-held blue or white flower heads give colour during summer. The dwarf forms take a little longer to establish in these harsh conditions but give a gentler appearance with their finer strappy leaves.

- Pave the offending area and to give it a purpose, add a garden seat, or if you prefer, a garden setting. If the paving looks a bit stark, a few pavers or occasional flagstones can be left out and filled with shade-tolerant ground cover plants. Many ground covers, such as Australian violet (*Viola hederacea*), also stand root competition.

- Or, go further with the ground cover and confine paving to a patch in front of the seat. Add a few stepping stones so the seat is defined and easily reached through the ground cover, which is best chosen from among those plants which reach no more than ankle height. Some form of mower

# Shrubs for Shaded Areas

P = adaptable to part sun    F = adaptable to full sun

| Common name | Botanical name | Details | Code |
|---|---|---|---|
| | *Abutilon megapotamicum* | delicate red and yellow bell-like flowers | F |
| Camellias: | | | |
| | *Camellia japonica* | unlikely to flower in deep shade | P |
| | *Camellia sasanqua* | unlikely to flower in deep shade | F |
| | *Corylopsis pauciflora* | bears fragrant, pale yellow flowers | P |
| | *Elaeagnus pungens* 'Maculata' | hardy, easy-care shrub | F |
| | *Fatsia japonica* | shapely large shiny, green leaves | P |
| Fuchsia | *Fuchsia* species | wide range of species and hybrids | P |
| | *Strobilanthes atropurpureus* | small mauve flowers | P |
| Hydrangea | *Hydrangea macrophylla* | needs good light to flower well | P |
| | *Hypericum calycinum* | semi-deciduous, yellow summer flowers | F |
| | *Aucuba japonica* | large, glossy, green leaves | F |
| | *Leucothoe fontanesiana* | dark-green foliage with sprays of small pearl-like flowers | P |
| Lily of the valley shrub | *Pieris japonica* | of neat habit, likes moist, acidic soil | P |
| | *Lonicera pileata* | makes good ground cover | P |
| | *Mahonia japonica* | sprays of fragrant yellow flowers throughout winter | P |
| Maple | *Acer palmatum* | many cultivars in Dissectum Group with fine leaves | |
| Heavenly bamboo | *Nandina domestica* | upright, elegant shrub, purplish-red foliage in autumn/winter | |
| | *Pieris floribunda* | white blooms from early spring | P |
| | *Potentilla fruticosa* 'Red Ace' | bright vermillion flowers | P |
| | *P. f.* 'Sunset' | deep orange flowers | P |
| Rhododendron | *Rhododendron* species | many species in a myriad of colours (also called 'Azaleas') | |
| | *Skimmia japonica* varieties | all have attractive foliage and carry colourful berries | P |
| Tree fern | *Dicksonia antarctica* | does best in sheltered, moist position | |
| | *Viburnum davidii* | deep-green oval leaves with heads of tiny white flowers | P |
| | *Vinca major* 'Variegata' | green leaves edged with creamy-white | P |
| | *Zenobia pulverulenta* | bears fragrant, white flowers in summer | P |

LEFT: *Hardy foxgloves* Digitalis purpurea *will often self-seed in a garden to provide spires of colour even in areas where they have to compete with tree roots.*

strip between ground cover and grass is also desirable to stop one running into the other. A nook like this with a seat not only eliminates a dreary area and adds interest, but gives the garden a friendlier, welcoming atmosphere. Also, you will appreciate how nice it is to have a shady place to relax in the garden during summer.

• Accentuate the shade and the feeling of coolness by putting in a ready-made fibre-glass pond, surrounded by mossy rocks and a variety of ferns. Ferns do need water but not as much as is generally considered necessary; once established in the garden they don't need the frequent watering they do in containers.

This project should be carried out during the winter months and the ferns planted in late winter or early spring to ensure that the ferns get established successfully.

**Key**

1. Pink flowering cherry (*Prunus serrulata* 'Kanzan')
2. Tree fern (*Dicksonia antarctica*)
3. *Rhododendron* 'Blue Peter'
4. Chinese elm (*Ulmus parvifolia*)
5. *Ceanothus* 'Blue Pacific'
6. *Rosa* 'Nancy Hayward'
7. Golden chain tree (*Laburnum* x *watereri*)

As specimen trees grow their canopy changes a once sunny garden into a shaded oasis providing the gardener with a new challenge. One solution is to extend a path to form a shady sitting area. A shallow pond has been incorporated into this design and adds to the pleasure of sitting in this cool arbour.

6.

7.

# SUNNY SPOTS — HOT SPOTS FOR A MAKEOVER

*G*rass alternatives, in the form of paving or tough plants, are the answer for areas robbed of nourishment by tree roots where such areas are bathed in sunlight for most of the day as the sun creeps under the overhead canopy.

OPPOSITE: *While some of the existing garden was retained when an old house was replaced, the immediate area was given a makeover to take advantage of the many garden outlooks which the new house provided. This striking sun-bathed perennial border was the happy outcome beside a newly formed path leading to the mature shady garden.*

Just like their shady counterparts, those barren sunny areas where lawns once flourished are ideal for adding paving and a seat. However, there are many other alternatives that are also worth considering.

Construct a garden, preferably on the same level as the lawn or, if not, built up no more than a few centimetres, otherwise the tree roots can suffocate. A bed flush with the lawn often looks better but may need a mower strip to prevent an area forming where ground cover or gravel merges with grass. A mower strip is a good idea around any form of stone, brick or other soil retainer as it saves tedious clipping of the 'grass collar' that develops around it.

An area such as this will probably be too dry for annuals and many other flowering plants except Aurora daisies, gazanias and the various ice plants, once collectively known as mesembryanthemums, which are too lazy to open their flowers until the sun hits them.

Succulents can add a surprising amount of colour and tolerate long periods without water. They do not demand a sun-baked position as often imagined but foliage colour is better in about half sun, whether filtered by foliage or direct, and they flower better in the sun.

Just one of the thousands of species, or a grouping of say three or five different colours gives a more pleasing effect than trying to build up a botanical collection. For example, there are the buff golds of *Sedum adolphii* or *S. rubrotinctum* (also sold as *S. guatemalense*) with glossy green 'jellybean' foliage flushed in sunlight with reddish bronze, to choose two species from the 600 or so species of this one genus. There are about 300 crassulas with larger foliage ranging through soft blue-greys, lavenders, mauves, and pinks to creamy buff and bronze colours, some with erect clusters of bright flowers, others with gracefully pendulous bells.

The many species of agapanthus, as previously mentioned, are ideal for sunny situations with root competition.

Apart from different planting themes between the above groups, variety can be achieved by converting a large shrub or two with firm single or multiple trunks into small trees to provide shade for a seat and/or dwarf azaleas, ferns or any other of the plants listed for shade.

Seasonal colour can be enjoyed using bulbs and some perennials with low maintenance, by planting them below a carpet of weed-retarding ground cover.

I successfully grow bluebells among a carpet of Australian violets (*Viola hederacea*) in a root-infested area under an Atlantic cedar. The same combination would also suit a damp area. Australian violets are evergreen but they are conveniently at their lowest ebb when the bluebells are flowering, then, as the foliage of the latter dies off, they spring back into new growth to cover the foliage which has died down. Efficient recycling, saving me the trouble of removing it.

Other bulbs such as daffodils and scillas can also be planted this way, as they push through the ground cover happily when ready. In a shaded area, I enjoy gentle drifts of snowdrops (*Galanthus* species) as they push up through a cover of variegated ivy. In the early spring, the pure white of the snowdrops is set off to advantage by the cream variegation of the ivy; this variegation then adds light and interest to the area throughout the remaining seasons.

*Galanthus* 'S. Arnott' and *G.* 'Magnet' are ideal, with handsome, bold flowers standing well above the ivy; the former having the additional attraction of being scented

A small, not too-obtrusive statue looking into a pond or amongst ferns would add charm to such an area, as long as there is shade from the afternoon summer sun.

See also: Rejuvenating an Old Lawn, p 109, Compacted Garden Soil, p 45, and Ground Covers – The Answer to Weed Control, p 88.

LEFT AND BELOW: *The use of old bricks, tumbling ground covers and low-growing shrubs provide an easy-care solution for sunny gardens. Full sun also provides a position where a rose such as 'Crepescule' can thrive and bloom to perfection.*

# WHY NEW PLANTS FAIL

I n trying to add interest to a mature garden, new plants may be added to an established border. However, there are reasons why extra care is needed to ensure success when new plants have to compete for moisture and nourishment.

BELOW: *In semi-shaded gardens, where many plants are competing for the available nutrients under the trees, Clematis 'Nelly Moser' will happily scramble along the ground and up the trunk of trees, providing spectacular colour and interest.*

Over the life of a garden new plants may have been added to bring life and interest into the garden. These are usually planted in front of the borderline shrubbery, or an old shrub may have been taken out and replaced with another. These newcomers, apart from other shrubs, may be roses, perennials or even annuals. They looked fairly happy for a while, perhaps made new growth, but then they slowed down to become stagnant and actually detracted from the garden.

This can be because the plants became root-bound, sometimes while the gardener was waiting to find or to prepare a place to suit them. During this extended time in a pot, the roots have been circling the pot in desperation, making a woody mass of fibrous roots around its side. This seems to lock them into a continual spiral, because when transplanted to the garden in this state, they may make a little growth initially then slow down, perhaps to die during a hot dry spell because the plant has no means of searching for water.

There is also a similar factor known as 'interface' which occurs when a plant with reasonably healthy roots is planted in soil much less attractive to it than that in the nursery container. The roots simply refuse to move from their original soil ball and virtually become root-bound as a result.

In both cases, it is necessary to unravel roots and, starting from the base up, spread and cover the roots, layer by layer, with the backfill of the planting hole which has been improved by the addition of about a third of its volume of well-rotted compost or animal manure.

Another reason why new plantings fail in old gardens is due to kindness and a determination to make them prosper. They are given improved soil, or at least mulched, and watered frequently. The old established ones that are expected to fend for themselves, sense that there is a good thing going on nearby, and lose no time in sending their roots into the favoured spot. Naturally, the poor little newcomers then have more root competition than ever, leaving them incapable of living up to expectations.

The answer is not to let the newcomers fend for themselves but for the first few months at least to water as wide an area as possible. Then later in the active growing season, when a manure or plant food would speed progress, to feed a wide area. In fact, it can help to reduce this root competition problem to place a few decoys away from the newcomers, within old shrubbery or trees. Root attractants such as slight depressions filled with compost or a handful or so of fertiliser trickled in with the hose will soon have established roots foraging within their moist richness.

On this theme, it can be appreciated that your hose 'accidently' watering over the fence, or a handful or two of fertiliser blowing over, will help to keep your neighbours' tree roots from invading your garden!

Incidently, when you do spend money on plant foods, do so when the plants can use them, which is when they are starting to make new growth, which is usually in spring, or just after flowering for the spring-flowering shrubs. Otherwise, most of the plant foods can be leached or washed out of the soil by the time the plants need them. If you have been over-generous, you can do more harm than good, especially with azaleas, daphnes, kalmias, ericas (all of which have a mat of fine roots very near the soil surface) and plants which have evolved in nutrient-poor soils.

# Why Plants Fail

1.

**1.** If plants are left too long in containers they become pot-bound. That is, spiralling roots form a dense mass and these will continue to circle when the plant is placed in the ground and eventually lead to the death of the plant.

2.

**2.** Before planting, soak the pot for 15 minutes to help ease the plant out of the container. Then carefully remove the plant from the pot and gently tease out most of the tangled, very long roots, cutting off any that are broken or damaged.

3.

**3.** Dig a hole with plenty of room at the sides and base of the plant to allow for healthy growth. Fill layer by layer with backfill from the hole enriched to about a third of its volume with compost or manure.

# RECTIFYING COMPACTED SOIL

Compacted soil inhibits plant growth by not allowing air, and often water, to penetrate. Luckily it is easy to rectify these problems in both lawns and gardens once we understand the mechanics of soil health.

Compacted soil is often the result of walking or other pressure on the soil when wet. The soil particles are pressed closer together, closing the tiny spaces between them which normally allow oxygen (and water) to enter. Plant growth fails or is poor in compacted soil because entry of oxygen essential for healthy root functioning has been greatly reduced or excluded.

While on the subject of oxygen and spaces between soil particles, it can also be seen that oxygen cannot enter, or toxic gases escape, when these spaces are filled with water. This is why soil drainage is important. Plant roots in soils saturated for long periods are unable to take in water, even though immersed in it. Therefore some form of drainage helps to minimise soil compaction. There are easy-to-lay, flexible types of drainage pipe available, usually with easy-to-follow instructions for installing them.

## COMPACTED LAWNS

Apart from fixing drainage, compacted soil can be corrected in lawns by driving a standard garden fork in every 10–12 cm (4–5 in) and a similar distance apart. Use a slightly lifting action and move the fork back and forth a little to widen the hole. Then if possible brush in a little fibrous compost — even dried-out grass clippings — to help keep the holes open. There are also hollow-tined forks that can be hired to draw out a small core of soil, leaving holes which accept compost more readily.

Compacted areas in lawns are more commonly caused by walking on the soil while it is wet, which at times is unavoidable. Good root growth of the grass helps to offset the adverse effects of this but eventually the treatment mentioned in the preceding paragraph may be needed.

Worst-affected areas occur where constant traffic also bruises or wears the grass. Remember that people instinctively take the shortest route; widening or replanning a path can eliminate the need to cut corners.

A worn track across a lawn or garden indicates the need for a path. Where a path would spoil the general effect by interrupting the generous flowing appearance of the lawn, stepping stones are a less obtrusive alternative and still prevent most of the wear. They are often the answer in places where a lawn narrows and therefore concentrates the traffic, or where it is tempting to cross say from patio to path. Stepping stones may be placed in the garden anywhere you need to step or stand for garden maintenance and at the same time they can add interest.

Where a comparatively narrow corner of the garden is set aside for design purposes, it can be prevented from becoming a compacted 'no-man's land' by corner cutting, if given an obvious reason for being there. A birdbath, a small (but uncomfortable to step over) shrub, a rock feature, statue or other object, can subtly act as a deterrent to straying feet.

## COMPACTED GARDEN SOIL

This is an easier problem to rectify. After a shower of rain or hosing, when the soil has dried out or is just damp, spread a layer of compost or even a thin layer of sawdust over the surface. If it is a clayey soil, then fork it in to a depth of 15–20 cm (6–8 in), less if you come to a tight unyielding clay subsoil. Then when the soil has been reasonably broken up, protect it from heavy rain or watering by spreading 3–4 cm (1–1½ in) of fibrous compost or leaf mould.

Before planting, give the garden two to three weeks to settle down. Rake the surface mulch back sufficiently to add new plants, then, when each planting is completed, return it, preferably before watering. Be sure when raking the compost around plants to keep slightly back from the trunk or stem so as not to 'burn' the plant tissues — this is especially pertinent when using bought mulch which has not yet decayed or broken down.

It should be noted that while sawdust is effective to lighten heavy or sticky clayey soils, like undecomposed shavings, woodchip or leaves dug into the soil, it does take nitrogen from the soil while decomposing. Unless complete fertiliser, fowl manure or similar nitrogenous material is added, plantings made during this period may show poor growth. This does not apply when any of these organic materials are used only as a surface mulch, as they then take the nitrogen needed for decomposition from the air.

On heavy clay soils this mulching is a continuing process which eventually helps to make the soil more friable. Adding a top-up layer of mulch is best repeated at least once a year. Before spreading the new load, lightly dig the remains of last season's mulch into the soil — you will notice the difference in the soil texture within a year or two. Some gardeners like to use the same type of mulch; others prefer to alternate with various materials.

Soil unprotected by leaf mould or plants will develop a hard crusty surface when it dries out after heavy rain or watering, more so if dug, planted, weeded or disturbed in other ways before it has dried out to the just damp state.

ABOVE: *Adding compost to compacted garden beds is the quickest and most effective way to reinvigorate the soil. Compost bins made from bales of straw can provide bonus compost as the moistened bales are pushed into the centre as they break down, with new bales added to the outside.*

# ELIMINATING WEED GROWTH

I t doesn't take long for some plants to escape the bounds of good behaviour to become virtual weeds. Rid the garden of these problem plants before the makeover begins and you're well on the way to an easy-care garden.

Most grassy and broad-leafed weeds can be eliminated by spraying to wet the foliage with glyphosate. This is sold under various trade names (ask at your local garden centre). Brands vary considerably in strength of glyphosate content, so be sure to read the label to check recommended dilution rate and apply as directed, remembering that special care needs to be taken to avoid contact with eyes and skin by wearing protective clothing and gloves. Also spray when there is no wind, as spray drift can be harmful to you, pets and wanted plants.

Most weeds die within about three weeks from treatment, after which time soil may be replanted. Some perennial weeds may need a second application. Results are best when weeds are in active growth.

Annual weeds such as summer grass, winter grass, chickweed, fat hen, thistles or clovers can be killed by just scuffling the surface early on a hot dry or windy day. More persistent perennials like buttercup, which do not produce underground runners or bulbs, can be eliminated during these conditions by cutting just below their woody crown, as actual roots will not regenerate. In the case of a large or very overgrown neglected area, any persistent perennial weeds like couch grass (twitch) or dandelions will need to be removed. This can be done by spraying with one of the glyphosate preparations when weeds are in active growth, which, in most cases, is during the warmer weather when soil is moist. Avoid spray drift or run-off near wanted plants, especially roses. In a couple of weeks after the weeds have been successfully killed, it is worth watering the area thoroughly to encourage regrowth from dormant weed seeds and underground runners. Spray again if necessary.

Where weeds meet shrubs, trees and perennials, spraying almost up to these plants is usually safe providing only enough spray is used to wet weeds without causing run-off into soil. Here again, it is imperative to shield wanted plants from spray drift.

Persistent bulbous weeds like oxalis can be very time-consuming and difficult to eradicate by hand. Destruction of the foliage, by hand or with chemicals, stimulates the ripening of the underground bulbils, which makes the plants increase all the faster. The best method in a heavily infested area is to choke the weeds using wads of newspaper or old carpet, which in turn can be covered with surface mulch. On a smaller scale, thorough hand-weeding will be successful. Ensure that the weed is incinerated

OPPOSITE: *Prostrate conifer cultivars are one of the best methods of inhibiting weeds as they provide a thick mat of ground-hugging dense and tidy growth.*

and not incorporated into the compost.

Bracken is capable of spreading extensively by means of its underground rhizomes and often proves extremely difficult to eradicate. Repeatedly breaking off the young fronds as they emerge will certainly help to curtail the spread.

Timing is of key importance. Aim to eradicate the offending weeds before they have time to seed and so re-establish their presence for another season. Faced with a cohort of dock (*Rumex*), and lacking the time to dig out each plant individually, or unable to spray beacause of the weather conditions, take time to snip off the flower heads before the seeds ripen. This will slow down the invasion and give you time to counter-attack with a chemical preparation.

Runaway vines can also pose a problem. Ornamental vines are useful for screening fences or unwanted views. The deciduous types, especially ornamental grape and wisteria, are practical as trellis or pergola covers to provide welcome summer shade and also allow sunlight to penetrate during their deciduous winter period. However, they can outrun their welcome as a garden matures.

Wisteria, pink jasmine, ivy and vines with colourful trumpet flowers formerly grouped under bignonias soon become invasive if their numerous canes are allowed to travel along the ground. Then they rapidly self-layer, make deep roots and soon form an unwanted tangle of growth that is difficult to eradicate.

Deal with this problem by isolating and staking upwards a few of the canes where they may be matted (in case you finally decide that they are wanted). Then, providing they are still in foliage, spray to wet all parts of the unwanted remainder with one of the glyphosate preparations suggested earlier for weed control. A possibly safer and more economical alternative is to scrape away some tissue from these grouped layers and immediately paint with the preparation, allowing the plant's sap to transport the chemical. A second or even a third treatment may be needed the following season, especially for wisteria, as roots or well-established layers may well regrow. Jasmine and some of the various trumpet-flowering vines can be eliminated by digging to cut the fibrous roots just below where growth emerges from the self-layered canes.

Brambles may appear the most foreboding invader, but with strong gloves, and with arms and legs protected from the thorny branches, it can be easily cut back to the lower stems and treated with glyphosate. When digging up the root, ensure you remove it in its entirety, as those roots that remain snapped below soil level are likely to re-grow , with added determination.

Nettles grow well in nitrogen-rich soil and so, whilst initially undesirable, they are harbingers of good, indicating excellent soil for further cultivation. Arm yourself with strong gloves and with arm and leg protection, and they are fairly easy to uproot. Add them to your compost and you will return the nitrogen back into the soil.

Make the invaders work for you. Mulching is a vital aspect of restoring health to soil that has long been neglected. By returning much of the unwanted growth to garden beds in the form of a surface layer, digging, weeding and watering will be reduced to a minimum.

It is more satisfying to get rid of cleared-away growth and show off the results of your labour, but in the long run it is kinder to you if this rubbish (apart from anything likely to resprout) is spread to deter the all-too-rapid growth of unwanted weeds that follow when the earth is suddenly exposed. It is also kinder to your soil, both as a mulch to improve its physical qualities and during decomposition to return the nutrients it removed during growth.

If you can't stand the sight of this or are eager to replant the area, either put the spent mulch through a shredder or spread an alternative mulch such as woodchip, pine bark

LEFT: *The aim of a gardener looking to establish an easy-care garden with a minimum of weed growth is to cover the bare earth with low-branching shrub species. Their natural low and neat habit can be further enhanced by lightly trimming new spring growth. If only one or two shrubs are involved, tip prune by hand; otherwise, use shears to create a neat dome effect.*

or leaf mould. Several layers of newspapers spread before laying the mulch will increase its weed-retarding properties.

Weed mats of woven plastic or fibre are also available. These generally stop the growth of most weeds but still allow penetration of water to the soil. Plants may be introduced by making buttonhole type cuts in the sheeting or raking away only as much as necessary of friable mulch, and raking it back as close as possible to the stem or trunk afterwards, remembering to leave a slight space between mulch and trunk.

Once grown for its autumn foliage, the Rhus tree (*Toxicodendron succedaneum*) is now often listed as a noxious plant because of the serious allergies associated with it. As contact with its sap can be dangerous, it is advisable to wait until the tree is dormant then, wearing protective clothing, dig up as much of the stump as possible; alternatively, chop the tree down to the stump and slash with an axe, then apply a strong solution of glyphosate.

There are other serious invaders of older gardens, particularly privet, holly and elder. These shrubs self-sow freely and are easily overlooked as, once grown to a reasonably self-assured height, they give the impression of belonging. Don't be intimidated – isolate the offenders and remove them.

Self-sown invaders up to about a metre (3 ft) high can often be pulled out when the soil is moist down to the subsoil. It is best to grub out larger specimens entirely.

If the grubbing is too difficult, these self-sown invaders can be killed by cutting them down close to ground level then making a few cuts on the remaining stump. While they are still damp and sappy, paint the cuts, particularly the top area, with a strong solution of glyphosate.

Should any suckers develop later, paint or spray these with the same chemical. If rain is imminent, cover the stump with a plastic bag or something else that is waterproof, so that the rain does not dilute the glyphosate.

# rejuvenation

## LET THE

## RENEWAL BEGIN

# TREES AND SHRUBS — GARDEN STYLE SETTERS

W hether the mature garden has existing trees or you intend moving or adding new ones, there are practical aspects to be considered to ensure success.

For maximum comfort, the ideal is to achieve a plan where verandas, windows and other outdoor living areas enjoy winter sun and cool shade in summer.

Before finalising positions for planting trees or large shrubs, drive a two-metre (6 ft) stake into the proposed planting site. View this from all positions, from both inside and outside the house, visualising the width and height of your chosen tree when centred there.

Deciduous trees are commendable because most give fairly dense shade in summer while during winter there is only a light dappling of shade from bare branches. There may be complaints from people who do not yet appreciate the value of leaves to a garden, grumbling that 'they make such a mess' but leaves should be seen as part of the garden.

The objectors may not realise that all but jacarandas and a few other trees from warmer climates make the one glorious leaf drop after their autumn colour finishes. Evergreens, including gum trees, are shedding leaves throughout the year, especially during hot dry spells in summer.

Irrespective of when trees drop leaves, any relatively high-branching tree can be positioned near the living areas of a house so that the low-angled winter sun penetrates below its branches, while during summer, when sun is higher in the sky, it throws shade more directly below, where it is appreciated.

If you are fortunate enough to have an established tree in a position where it gives summer shade where needed, the lower branches may be trimmed off to also allow winter sun to penetrate where it is wanted.

Another point not often considered in defence of deciduous trees is that in their leafless winter stage, if viewed without prejudice, most have great character in trunk and branches. They throw a delightful tracery on walls and lawns in addition to providing stark silhouettes against the winter sky.

Shadows are another element that can give a garden charm and interest. They vary according to time of day and help define the seasons.

Similarly, deciduous trees reflect seasonal change, displaying beautifully fresh silk-like pale green or velvety copper leaves in early spring, which spread and thicken to a welcome shady canopy in summer. Then their autumn finale starts with a soft golden glow that gradually bursts into bright copper and fiery red, before departing to provide mulch ready to feed next spring's outburst of growth.

If planning to use or replant trees, it's worth avoiding cedars (*Cedrus atlantica*, *C. deodara* or *C. libani* and their cultivars) overhanging outdoor living areas, pools, driveways and paths. Although very ornamental, they continually shed needle-like leaves that block pool filters and are readily transported on clothing, damp soles of shoes, etc, finding their way indoors and onto car mats and upholstery. This can cause much discomfort!

Gardeners do not always appreciate the ultimate width of trees. For example, the popular liquidambar can ultimately develop a spread of 15–23 m (50–75 ft). Many cultivars of popular tree species have been developed to suit the ever-decreasing size of suburban gardens. Although height and width do vary with soil and climate conditions, the following lists will give readers a guide as to dimensions.

## MINIMISING ROOT DAMAGE

The suggestion of trees near houses naturally raises the question of possible root damage. Some trees, including liquidambars, develop a heavy root system and should be kept at least 7 m (23 ft) from foundations. There is no set rule because roots will travel more readily to wherever the soil is dampest, which should not be below the house unless drainage is faulty. In fact, to ensure greater safety, it is now possible to install a permanent irrigation drip a few metres (feet) out from the trunk on the opposite side to building foundations or even from paved areas.

Where there is a danger of surface roots lifting paved or concrete paths or terraces, a trench 50–70 cm (1½–2 ft) out from paths and terraces and dug to the same depth, lined nearly to the top with heavy-gauge

# Deciduous Shade Trees for Small Gardens

H = maximum height     W = maximum width

| Common name | Botanical name | Details | H | W |
|---|---|---|---|---|
| Contorted willow | *Salix babylonica* var. *pekinensis* 'Tortuosa' | curled branches evident when dormant | 12 m (40 ft) | 8 m (25 ft) |
| Crab-apple | *Malus floribunda* | masses of apple-pink blossom in spring, | 9 m (28ft) | 10 m (30 ft) |
| | *M.* x *purpurea* | bronze-purple foliage | 8 m (25 ft) | 10 m (30 ft) |
| Crape myrtle | *Lagerstroemia indica* | late summer flowers, autumn colouring plus beautiful bark | 6 m (20 ft) | 5 m (16 ft) |
| Flowering peach | *Prunus persica* | winter/spring-flowering cultivars; prune back hard after flowering to avoid fruit fly problems | 5 m (16 ft) | 4 m (12 ft) |
| Flowering plums: | *Prunus cerasifera* 'Pissardii' | with deep purple foliage | 10 m (30 ft) | 10 m (30 ft) |
| | *P.* x *blireana* | early double pale-pink blossoms | 4 m (12 ft) | 4 m (12 ft) |
| Golden elm | *Ulmus procera* 'Louis van Houtte' | a citrus-yellow cultivar of English elm | 10 m (30 ft) | 10 m (30 ft) |
| Golden honey locust | *Gleditsia triacanthos* 'Sunburst' | quick-growing with golden foliage | 10 m (30 ft) | 5 m (16 ft) |
| Golden rain tree | *Koelreuteria paniculata* | although slow-growing it forms a wide canopy | 10 m (30 ft) | 10 m (30 ft) |
| Persian ironwood | *Parrotia persica* | autumn leaves hold well | 7 m (22 ft) | 10 m (30 ft) |
| Japanese cherry | *Prunus serrulata* | various cultivars provide glorious spring blossom | 10 m (30 ft) | 10 m (30 ft) |
| Japanese elm | *Zelkova serrata* | has a wide, spreading habit | 10 m (30 ft) | 10 m (30 ft) |
| Japanese maple | *Acer palmatum* | good autumn colour | 6 m (20 ft) | 6 m (20 ft) |
| Rowan | *Sorbus aucuparia* | best for cool to cooler temperate areas | 12 m (40 ft) | 6 m (20 ft) |
| Taiwan or bell cherry | *Prunus campanulata* | with long clusters of slender purplish bells in late winter (not for severe frosts) | 8 m (25 ft) | 8 m (25 ft) |
| Trident maple | *Acer buergerianum* | interesting-shaped leaves that colour well | 10 m (30 ft) | 8 m (25 ft) |

# Evergreen Shade Trees for Small gardens

H = maximum height     W = maximum width

| Common name | Botanical name | Details | H | W |
|---|---|---|---|---|
| **Conifers:** | | | | |
| | *Cedrus deodara* 'Aurea' | yellowish-green, pendent foliage | 5 m (16 ft) | 4 m (12 ft) |
| | *Chaemaecyparis obtusa* 'Crippsii' | aromatic, bright golden foliage | 10 m (30 ft) | 5 m (16 ft) |
| | *Juniperus recurva* | aromatic, blue-green leaves | 10 m (30 ft) | 6 m (20 ft) |
| Cotoneaster | *Cotoneaster frigidus* | vigorous and quick to grow | 10 m (30 ft) | 10 m (30 ft) |
| | *C. serotinus* | brilliant red berries | 6 m (20 ft) | 6 m (20 ft) |
| **Eucalyptus:** Snow gum | *E. pauciflora* | patchwork-like, flaking bark | 10 m (30 ft) | 6 m (20 ft) |
| Spinning gum | *E. perriana* | fast-growing, attractive tree | 7 m (22 ft) | 4 m (12 ft) |
| **Hollies:** | | | | |
| | *Ilex aquifolium* varieties | attractive foliage and berries | 14 m (46 ft) | 6 m (20 ft) |
| | *Ilex purpurea* | lavender flowers are followed by scarlet fruits | 12 m (40 ft) | 6 m (20 ft) |
| | *Photinia davidiana* | glossy, green leaves; bright red fruits in autumn | 7 m (22 ft) | 5 m (16 ft) |

plastic sheeting, tends to direct roots downwards, which should be too deep to cause any damage.

Should you need to lay new piping close to an established tree, the least damage is done to the fragile root system by tunnelling directly under the trunk. Cutting the tap root, if it still exists, is not important.

## HIGH-BRANCHING TREES

For obvious reasons, it is as well to avoid trees such as eucalypts or oaks that may develop heavy limbs overhanging houses. Certainly, trees do drop occasional branches, especially while the mature trunks are forming. Sometimes mature limbs fall from old trees. However, contrary to reputation, many species of trees only drop limbs when they are placed under stress. Trees can be severely stressed if their main roots have been cut by trenching for foundations, for the laying of underground services or the like, or where paving such as concrete, bitumen or other solid cover has been laid close enough to prevent water from reaching the roots. This has a smothering effect similar to what happens when the flow of air to surface roots is restricted when a change of soil level occurs due to remodelling or extension of a house.

# MOVING TREES OR SHRUBS

*O*ften quite large plants are needlessly sacrificed when a house extension is to take place. With a little planning, this need not happen. With careful preparation throughout the previous season, many precious specimens will flourish in their new position.

Many trees and shrubs can be moved successfully during the winter dormant period. One exception is that warmth-lovers, such as the evergreen hibiscus, are best left until late winter to early spring when severe frosts are less likely. It should also be noted that, some are more sensitive to root disturbance and are therefore less likely to survive the move. Plants less likely to prove amenable to transplanting include daphne, proteas, acacias and eucalypts; when moving such plants it's a good idea to take cuttings (in warmer months) or collect seed when ripe, to ensure that a favourite plant is not lost in case the move is unsuccessful.

Most roses and deciduous caney shrubs, such as weigela, May (*Spirea cantoniensis*), dwarf prunus, hydrangeas, Guelder rose (*Viburnum opulus*) and other deciduous viburnums can be moved easily when the soil is damp during their winter dormant period.

It is usually sufficient just to trench down 15 to 20 cm (6 to 8 in) beyond their outer canes to about the depth of a spade, then dig under them until the root ball can be levered out. Cleanly recut any broken or burred roots.

Replant before roots or soil dry out, making the plants' holes in their new location only a few centimetres (about one inch) deeper than their root ball but at least half as wide again so that well-composted or crumbly top soil can be added to encourage new root growth.

Prune back to compensate for reduced root growth. It may be easier to do this just before the move to minimise damage.

Water in well. If possible, spread a 3 cm (1 in) mulch of still-fibrous compost, partly rotted grass clippings or leaves, especially over the added soil, if possible before watering, as this will deter soil from caking and speed new root regeneration.

Some form of temporary support like staking may be needed to prevent root movement. Props

## ENCOURAGING NEW ROOTS

*The soil filled back around the roots should be as good as that in which the plant grew previously, otherwise new roots may be reluctant to venture into their new site. Improve it by adding one-third well-rotted leaf mould to two-thirds existing soil.*

# Moving Trees and Shrubs

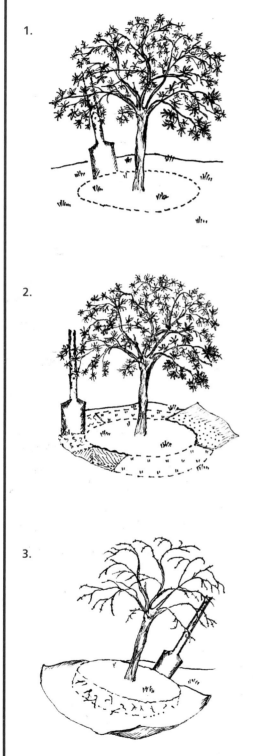

**1.**

**1.** Quite large shrubs can be moved successfully if a few guidelines are followed. About six months before the move, begin by marking a circle approximately three times the radius of the trunk's thickness out from its base.

**2.**

**2.** Divide this circle into sections and trench each alternate section, cutting roots cleanly. Cover any exposed roots with plastic sheeting and backfill with the soil to hold it in position. Three months later, dig the remaining sections in the same manner.

**3.**

**3.** When the plant is dormant, dig a wider area out from the trench to gain good access to the roots underneath the trunk. Work a tarpaulin under the root ball as the roots are cut to facilitate the move.

or crossover stakes from either side of the root ball are preferable to a single upright one that penetrates the root ball.

Established maples, crape myrtles and other single-stemmed specimens in the shrub rather than tree category can be moved by making the root ball size about equivalent in width to that of the plant when pruned back. Replant as above.

## TRANSPLANTING WELL-ESTABLISHED SPECIMENS

Setback or failure when moving a large shrub or tree is greatly reduced by conditioning it well in advance of the move which ideally should take place while the plant is dormant. That is in early winter for deciduous trees in temperate areas and late winter to early spring in cold, wet areas. Evergreens are also best transplanted during the cooler months. Preferably start about six months before the move by marking a circle about three times the radius of the trunk thickness out from its base. Divide this circle into four or even six sections or segments. Spade down to trench each alternate segment, cutting or sawing the large roots cleanly. Having the trench wide enough to continue in as far as possible under the tree makes the task easier.

As each trench is completed, cover the exposed roots with a piece of plastic and

## MOVING CONIFERS

*Late autumn is the best time for replanting; if possible, make the soil ball nearly as wide as the foliage spread. If necessary, the foliage spread may be reduced, providing some leaves are retained on all branches (but not leading shoot). Bear in mind, though, that some conifers take a long time to make new growth.*

carefully fill back the soil to hold it. As a further refinement, while doing this, I like to trickle in a little well-rotted compost, or a mixture of either crumbly or sandy soil and compost, to make a layer a few centimetres (one inch) thick between root ball and plastic. This helps to form a layer of new fibrous roots over the cut section.

After about three months, trench the remainder of the root ball and treat similarly to the first ones. Alternatively, if weather is still cool and the tree or large shrub is still dormant, the move may be completed by trenching completely around the earlier cuts, making the trench at least twice spade depth and nearly as wide, so that it can be extended as far as possible under the root ball to cut lower roots. Proceed until it is possible to rock the root ball so that a tarpaulin can be gradually worked under it. If this root ball is too heavy to lift with

a person on either side of the tarpaulin, then it should be secured with ropes around and below on either side. Then a ramp may be dug on a convenient side of the hole so that it can be rocked and dragged out. Here a sheet of roofing iron or planks will help it to slide out easily. An exceptionally heavy root ball can be manhandled more easily if strong timber shafts are secured to the ropes on either side.

Prepare the new position before you finally remove tree to reduce stress to a minimum. Once it has been transplanted, look for any damage to branches — some well-placed branches that are important to the overall shape of the tree may be able to be repaired by wrapping them in grafting tape or similar. However, if branches are badly broken, prune with sharp, clean secateurs or a pruning saw.

ABOVE: *Rather than transplanting, an established row of conifers has been given a softening, cottage garden effect by the additon of low-growing perennials and stepping-stone path. The naturally compact growth of many conifer cultivars can be further enhanced by a light overall prune.*

# PRUNING TREES AND SHRUBS

M ost trees and shrubs don't need regular pruning, but in an overgrown situation it is the quickest way to restore order to the garden. Don't let the idea of doing your own pruning scare you ... all you need is clean, sharp equipment.

OPPOSITE: *Nothing revives a garden quicker than giving many plants a prune. By keeping growth under control, it allows each plant to shine while blending shrubs of different growth habits together. With hydrangeas, however, breaking the rule of removing dead flowers results in a pleasing and continuing display of subtle colour throughout the winter months.*

Bad pruning or pruning at the wrong time rarely kills a shrub or tree. It usually means that the plant will not flower or flower sparsely for a season but these are faults most gardeners correct by trial and error.

So many gardeners, it seems, with secateurs in hand, are unable to resist the temptation to prune bare stemmed specimens like flowering peaches, other prunus, Guelder rose and weigela in winter. After all, the first two are winter-pruned in the orchard. However, this is done to increase fruit quality by minimising flowering and also to direct fruit-bearing into lower branches.

In the ornamental garden, the aim is for maximum flower display, therefore pruning is delayed until immediately after spring flowering. However, like most rules, there are exceptions, and pruning deciduous summer flowering shrubs is different.

## DECIDUOUS EARLY SPRING-FLOWERING SHRUBS

Shrubs with canes such as such as May (*Spiraea cantoniensis*), weigela, Guelder rose (*Viburnum opulus*), forsythia, kerria, deutzia are pruned as soon as possible after flowering.

Cut out old canes just above where a new cane is emerging or at ground level. Note that on an old neglected bush, the newer cane branching from it may also be in the 'old' category. Old canes can be identified by usually darker and rougher bark but more definitely by the fact that only comparatively thin twiggy growth is emerging from them. The newer canes are then shortened back, usually by about a third.

Deciduous magnolias are usually best left unpruned as they form natural attractive branching habits.

## FLOWERING FRUIT TREES.

Flowering fruit trees are also in the deciduous spring-flowering category. Crab-apples, pears, flowering cherries and plums need little

---

### PRUNING SHRUBS

A *light overall trim will induce more compact form where dense growth makes individual tip-pruning tedious. For example, azaleas and some tea-trees will respond to this method.*

---

# Low-branching Shrubs for Sun or Part-shade

P = Prune occasionally to keep low-branching habit
S = Prefers full sun, but adaptable

| Common name | Botanical name | Details | Code |
|---|---|---|---|
| Acer | *Acer palmatum* | year-round foliage interest | S |
| Azaleas | *Rhododendron* species | all the evergreen types ranging from dwarf to 1.5 m | P |
| Berberis: | | | |
| | *Berberis darwinii* | evergreen with bright yellow spring flowers | S |
| | *B. thunbergii* | reddish-purple foliage | S |
| Box | *Buxus microphylla* var. *japonica* | trim to desired shape, size | P |
| | *Brachyglottis monroi* | ideal for coastal areas | S |
| Brazilian bell flower | *Abutilon megapotamicum* | non-demanding plant seemingly always in flower | S |
| | *Ceanothus papillosus* or hybrids | ideal for a blue highlight | P |
| | *Choisya ternata* 'Sundance' | golden foliage | S |
| Cigar plant | *Cuphea ignea* | a compact foreground plant | P |
| | *Corylopsis pauciflora* | bears fragrant yellow flowers | P |
| | *Cotinus americanus* | attractive foliage year-round | P |
| | *C. coggygria* 'Royal Purple' | deep-purplish red foliage | P |
| Cotoneaster | *Cotoneaster horizontalis* | bears attractive, red fruits | S |
| | *Elaeagnus pungens* 'Maculata' | trouble-free plants with golden variegation to leaves | S |
| Heather | *Erica canaliculata* | has an open growth habits | P |
| | *Euonymus fortunei* 'Emerald 'n' Gold' | bright green leaves, margined with bright yellow and tinged pink in winter | S |
| | *Hebe* species | often called veronicas by older gardeners | S |
| | *Hypericum patulum* | golden-yellow flowers followed by red fruit | S |
| | *Juniperus procumbens* | low-growing conifer | S |
| | *Lonicera pileata* | makes good ground cover | P |
| | *Nandina domestica* 'Nana' | colours well as weather turns colder | |
| | *Prunus lusitanica* | reddish-purple shoots, bright green leaves, and white flowers | S |
| | *Rhaphiolepis umbellata* | tough plant with good coverage | |
| Rosemary | *Rosmarinus officinalis* | decorative and useful | S |
| | *Skimmia japonica* | aromatic leaves | P |

pruning, but if obviously old and neglected for some time, they can be rejuvenated by cutting back in winter to leave only the main framework of branches. This will naturally mean sacrificing flowers in the following spring. Excess spring growth following this heavy pruning will need rubbing off to leave only shoots pointing in the direction where new branches are wanted. Vigorous branches heading skywards can be curbed by pruning back in summer.

Flowering peaches are pruned more heavily than other deciduous ornamental fruits mentioned because they flower on wood made the previous spring and summer. Prune the canes that have flowered back to just above the bud at their base. This not only encourages canes densely packed with blossom the following spring but eliminates formation of fruit which is rarely particularly palatable.

One other exception in the prunus group is dwarf prunus (*P. glandulosa*). This is cut down to ground level after flowering to encourage a showy clump of blossom-packed canes the following year. Note that at one time budded or grafted plants of this species were sold. If in doubt, check that the woody bulbous bud union is not above ground. If so, prune to about 15 cm (6 in) above the latter.

## DECIDUOUS SUMMER-FLOWERING SHRUBS AND TREES

These are less numerous but include *Hibiscus syriacus*, vitex and crape myrtle (if it is kept as a shrub rather than a tree). These are

---

### RUBBING OFF

*The term rubbing off means just that — rubbing your thumb downwards along the branch to break off unwanted shoots.*

---

pruned back in winter to a stub about finger length, above where growth comes from a main branch.

One exception is hydrangeas, which are pruned back to just above the lowest set of plump double buds. However, in neglected gardens, these buds are likely to only occur high up on spindly branches. In this case, prune initially to just above any bud near the base of the plant. There will be few flowers in the main late-spring to summer flowering period but the orthodox pruning mentioned can then be started again the following winter.

Fuchsias are usually pruned in late winter, but in frost-free districts may be pruned when late summer flowers finish to encourage spring as well as summer flowers.

BELOW: *When branches obscure light from windows or overhang nearby paths, the answer is to prune low branches while the plant is dormant. Pruning slender branches is not only easier on the gardener, it also doesn't leave such an obvious scar on the tree trunk.*

*Buddleja davidii*, the well-known 'Butterfly Bush', will respond well to hard annual pruning. Neglected, this vigorous shrub will become leggy and a mass of tangled stems. This shrub flowers on new wood, so prune in the early spring, cutting out all the weak growth and congested stems, and shortening the new desired growth by one third. Note that some buddleja flower on old wood and need to be pruned accordingly. *B. alternifolia* should be pruned after flowering in midsummer, cutting back the stems to a healthy bud. Neglected specimens can be hard-pruned. *B. globosa* requires little pruning. Stems that bear the flowers too high for viewing can be cut back to the old wood during the winter.

## SUMMER-FLOWERING SHRUBS

These shrubs, including abelias, are pruned lightly after flowering, then heavily in winter. Treat abelias as spring-flowering caney shrubs, cutting out old canes.

The Himalayan honeysuckle, *Leycesteria formosa*, can be renovated by drastic pruning in the spring. Cut back all the stems to within 10–12 cm (4 in) from the base.

The popular Smoke bush, *Cotinus coggygria*, can be treated in two ways. If left unpruned, the shrub will produce billowing clouds of flowers in the summer months, which can be removed after flowering. If you wish, you can sacrifice these flowers for the luxury of the rich red colour of the leaves. An annual prune in the spring will dramatically increase leaf size.

The widely grown evergreen hibiscus love warmth and respond best to early spring pruning so that new growth is made while the weather is warming up. Cut back the vigorous canes made last season to leave about 20–35 cm (8–14 in) length, or even less for container-grown specimens. To some extent, growth can be controlled by cutting to just above a leaf pointing in the direction new growth is preferred. Tip-pruning will make the shrub more compact but delay flowering for five or six weeks. The lesser or

RIGHT: *When space is tight and you would like to cover a bare wall, the answer could be to train a suitable plant, such as the prunus illustrated, into an espalier. By careful pruning, wonderful effects can be created in traditional designs which are well-suited to deciduous plants. A rather more informal espalier can be used when working with evergreens as the bare framework of the design is not so evident.*

weaker canes may be left uncut to produce earlier flowers. Flowering is terminal (at the end of stem). Old plants may be cut back to main branches if necessary, but recovery may be slow.

Geraniums (Pelargoniums) of the widely grown zonal variety (with a horseshoe-like dark zone in leaf), and most others grown mainly for their flowers, are best pruned in winter or progressively as each stem ceases to carry flower buds. Coloured leaf types are usually pruned in early spring. Old stems carrying only weak growth are cut out at ground level; healthier canes are reduced by about a third. As new shoots reach about finger length or have made three or four leaves, pinch out the growing tip to encourage more growth. Continue until spring with flowering types or until coloured or fancy leafed types have made a compact plant.

Neglected geraniums or others becoming straggly are best renewed from 10–12 cm-long (4 in-long) tip cuttings which may be taken at pruning time. Start tip-pruning as suggested when growth commences.

## SPRING-FLOWERING SHRUBS

This represents the largest group of shrubs grown in cool to tropical districts, including exotics. Note that azaleas and camellias are dealt with individually on the following pages. Normal procedure is to cut back as soon as possible after flowering, preferably before new growth starts. Allow a few leaves to remain on each flower stem. Remove dead twigs or branches.

There are a few exceptions to the general type of pruning mentioned:

Daphne: Picking about one-third of the flowers is sufficient but not essential. New growth comes from the old flower head, so by picking the winter blooms you are effectively tip-pruning.

Lavender: Responds to fairly hard cutting as

flowering dwindles, usually in late-summer.

The Snowy Mespilus (*Amelanchier*): If treated as a single-stemmed specimen shrub, rub off the side-shoots that appear on the main trunk in the winter.

If renovation pruning is required, rather than, or in addition to, annual pruning, it is often best to carry out the task during the winter months, while the plant is still dormant.

## WINTER-FLOWERING SHRUBS

Chaenomeles (Flowering quince): In the summer shorten all the new growth to 5 or 6 leaves — this will dramatically improve flowering.

Chimonanthus: a free-standing specimen is best left unpruned. For a wall-trained shrub, cut out old branches in early spring.

Linum: Prune back to about 15 cm (6 in) after flowering has finished.

Mahonia: No regular pruning required. Stems which have become bare can be cut back in the spring to stronger growth.

Pieris: Trim off old flower heads, leaving a few leaves at the base of each stem. May be pruned harder if necessary to reduce height.

ABOVE: *Many types of shrubs and subshrubs, such as the dusty miller,* Senecio cineraria, *are all the better for regular tip-pruning. This not only encourages bushy growth which in turn produces more flowers. It can increase their garden life as a number of plants can otherwise become straggly making them prime targets for eviction in a general garden clean-up. Tip-prunings can be used to propagate favourite or short-lived plants.*

# CAMELLIAS — FIVE-STAR PERFORMERS

Camellias have wonderful landscape potential. They retain dark glossy foliage throughout the year, and in winter or spring provide a delightful array of appealing flowers. There is a wide choice of colour and form variety within each species.

Varieties of camellia and their hybrids are mostly in the shape of an upright pyramid with compact glossy elliptical or 'pointed oval' leaves 10–15 cm (4–6 in) in length. They flower mainly from late winter into late spring. While most varieties and hybrids perform best in dappled shade, there are a few that accept full sun. They are best suited to temperate districts with slightly acid, well-drained soil.

*Camellia sasanqua* varieties have smaller and unusually darker foliage than *C. japonica*. Most have more spreading growth but can be trimmed as hedges, domes, trained on walls as espaliers or be planted as a narrow cordon-like fence with interlaced branches trained to the one plane. They display a profusion of pink, white or red single or informal double flowers from mid-autumn to early winter. These grow in full sun or shade but are generally slower to progress and rarely flower appreciably in dense shade. They are more tolerant to alkaline soil than *C. japonica* varieties.

There are other camellia species of interest to garden enthusiasts including the yellow camellia *C. nitidissima* and the many newer hybrids with tiny blooms and graceful foliage.

## PRUNING CAMELLIAS

Pruning camellias need not be a yearly practice. Most *C. japonica* plants have naturally compact growth but picking blooms with one or two leaves left at the base of the flower stems helps to renew outer growth and usually the quality of next season's blooms. It also keeps plants more attractive by removing old blooms, although there are many 'self-grooming' varieties that shed them naturally.

## REJUVENATING CAMELLIAS

When *C. japonica* varieties have not been pruned after flowering for seven or eight years, they invariably make an excess of thin woody growth and flower quality deteriorates.

Rejuvenate during winter by removing all side growths thinner than a pencil on each branch, cutting it close to the branch. Then all remaining branchlets should be trimmed back to a point where they are at least pencil thickness. Any remaining foliage should be removed.

Early spring should bring an enthusiastic burst of new growth — usually too dense to make healthy new branchlets. Rub off surplus growth soon after it emerges to achieve an uncrowded even spacing of the remaining branchlets.

In the re-established garden where you may not care to sacrifice unopened flower buds or be

*OPPOSITE: Camellias provide a wall of green year round and delight with delicate blooms during the cooler months. A choice can be made between shade and sun-tolerant hybrids and between tall upright growers or those with a more bushy habit.*

prepared to endure the 'plucked' appearance for several weeks, a compromise is to treat half the main branches this way and the remainder the following year.

If camellias are too tall, there is no harm done by cutting back top branches just above a side branch at the height you prefer or a little lower. Later, either tip-prune or cut back shoots racing vertically.

Should you feel like treating the plants more drastically than indicated above, you will probably get away with it. Surprising as it may seem, I have seen camellias over 100 years old recover when the sizeable trunk has been sawn during winter to a stump 25 cm (10 in) high (admittedly under good growing conditions in a temperate climate)! *Camellia sasanqua* varieties may be cut heavily to the shape or size desired, preferably do this in early winter as the new growth starts (earlier than most *C. japonica* varieties).

However, note that different *C. sasanqua* varieties vary in growth habit. Many, like 'Setsugekka', 'Plantation Pink', 'Exquisite' and 'Lucinda', have spreading growth, growing to about 4 m (13 ft) and up to 3 m (10 ft) wide in 10 years and nearly twice that height eventually. 'Hiryu' makes fairly open caney upright growth more rapidly. However, it is easier to espalier or interlace as a freestanding cordon.

'Marie Young' gradually makes a slender but dense column usually less than 1 m (3 ft) across, whereas 'Shishi Gashira' and 'Sparkling Burgundy' rarely exceed 2 m (6 ft) in height and eventually a similar width. 'Pygmy' makes a dense dome usually less than 1 m (3 ft) high.

BELOW: Camellia sasanqua *'Hiryu' makes an ideal espalier plant. It is trained on a wall of rendered brick using horizontal wires placed 25 cm (10 in) apart.*

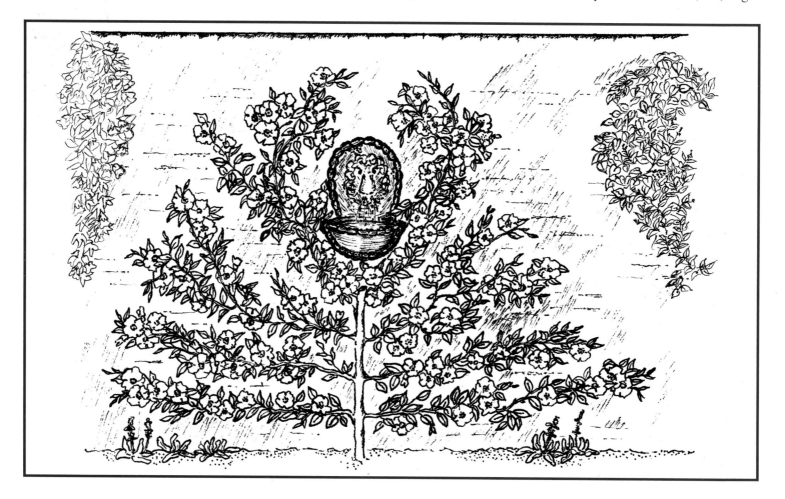

Then there is a range of miniatures for rockery or hanging basket planting with myriad tiny blooms to beguile.

Although the general range of *C. sasanquas* is easy to shape, you are ahead if you choose some that naturally grow in the form you prefer — appreciating that naturally smaller types will be more expensive because they take years longer to attain size in the nursery.

## MOVING CAMELLIAS

Camellias can be moved when dormant, before new growth buds begin unfolding — before flowering finishes. Young trees up to about 2 m (6 ft) can be moved when soil is damp by cutting down to about spade depth 15–18 cm (6–8 in) out from the trunk then lifting,

trimming roots cleanly then replanting no deeper than the previous depth except for a surface mulch of fibrous compost or rotted leaf mould, then given a gentle, prolonged soaking.

Larger camellias can be moved successfully following the procedure outlined under Moving Trees and Shrubs on p 58. The entire operation may be carried out during the winter dormant period without need for any conditioning providing that, immediately prior to moving it, the tree is pruned back severely, even though it may still be carrying flower buds.

You need willpower to forgo enjoying the immediate effect of the move but it will repay you later if the procedure on rejuvenating camellias (on the previous pages) is carefully followed. Successful pruning will pay dividends.

ABOVE: *Nothing brightens up a winter garden as much as a well-grown camellia in full bloom. Camellia 'Dr Clifford Parks' tolerates more sun than many camellias and blooms in mid-spring.*

# REJUVENATING AZALEAS PAST THEIR PRIME

Fashionable many years ago, azaleas are now more often than not waiting for a renewal program to provide many more years of colourful spring blossom.

 Many of the hybrid azaleas introduced mainly from the mid-1930s onwards, and the small-flowered Kurume types, are permanently compact unless growing in poor light, where they tend to elongate. Even so, they can be rejuvenated and kept still more compact by giving them an overall trim to remove some foliage and thin outer twiggy flower stems. This needs to be done as soon as the main early spring flowers finish and before new growth starts.

The older taller-growing azaleas, still widely grown for their spectacular spring flush of flowers, usually become leggy after 10 to 12 years and often carry their main show of flowers in a canopy above head height. These plants can be completely transformed into compact shapes in a surprisingly short time.

How? It seems ruthless and some may find it hard to do, but you have to saw all main stems down to about half their height or even lower — say about 20–25 cm (8–10 in) lower than the desired height over the next five years or so. This 'massacre' should be carried out as soon as flowers finish, certainly before new spring growth has started. If foliage is not infected with two-spotted mite or similar, save and shred or cut to use as mulch or compost.

Providing soil does not completely dry out, new growth should appear within a few weeks. When this reaches 10–15 cm (4–6 in) in length or has made four to six well formed leaves per stem, either pinch out the tip or, using shears, give a light overall trim. If the side shoots that follow gain this height before mid-summer, give a second trimming or tip-prune.

Tall sappy shoots that appear from lower down on the mature branches may be cut back a little below the general line of foliage.

Note that a very old azalea, especially if suffering from 'dieback', may not survive this heavy cutting — otherwise, chances of good recovery are at least nine out of ten.

When there are signs of new growth appearing after the rejuvenation pruning, a light

---

### DIEBACK

*Dieback is caused by a fungus disease but it can also be found where competition from overhanging foliage obstructs light and is evident when twiggy growth is easily snapped between fingers.*

ABOVE: *Sun-hardy 'Alphonse Anderson' trained as a standard azalea makes an eye-catching display in spring.*

BELOW: *Acid-loving plants, azaleas make ideal tub specimens where potted mix is used.*

decomposing natural leaf mould that collects over the soil below them. Also appreciate that as most of their roots are practically on the soil surface just below this leaf mulch, their food and water intake will be sadly depleted by so-called surface cultivation or other forms of digging.

The unattractive silver-grey mottling or bronzing of azalea leaves does not mean that the plants are diseased. This is caused by Azalea lace bug — a very small fly-like insect with comparatively large lacy wings that lies flat on the underside of the leaves and feeds on the green tissue. You will usually notice that azalea plants or parts of them most affected with lace bug damage are partly sheltered from the weather by overhanging trees or shrubs, eaves etc. Therefore, after an initial spraying with a systemic spray, the plants can be kept fairly free of lace bug by a weekly hosing with a jet of water strong enough to agitate the foliage. Like heavy rain, it dislodges these delicate creatures and they seem unable to return to the foliage.

feeding will help new growth to establish. Use an organic plant food or one of the complete water-soluble preparations — but also use restraint. More azaleas die due to overfeeding than from neglect as freely broadcast granular fertilisers can easily scorch both surface roots and foliage.

Many azaleas have been flourishing and flowering well for over 50 years on only water and nutrients provided entirely from the slowly

Tip-pruning or 'stopping' encourages more compact and bushy growth. As the name implies, it means pinching out the growing tip, usually done when the new shoot has made three or four sets of leaves, or a little below where you want a new growth to terminate. New shoots then come from the lower leaf junctions and stem. These new growths may be treated similarly if desired.

## TRANSPLANTING AZALEAS

Azaleas can be moved successfully from late autumn to early spring — even though they are in full flower — providing tender new growth has not started.

The main point to note is that azaleas make a comparatively wide and shallow mat of surface roots. Except for a few inconsequential deeper roots, this mat is rarely more than 12–15 cm (5–6 in) deep, and extending at least to below the outer rim of foliage.

LEFT: *Contrasting colour displays are possible with the various types of azaleas such as shown here, where a cool country Mollis type, available in a a wide range of yellows, combines with the more universal whites and pinks. Although azaleas are shallow-rooted, it is possible to combine annuals nearby if soil is nurtured and the area under their foliage is disturbed to a bare minimum.*

If the width involves too large a soil ball to handle, then prune the plant back to about half its size and reduce the soil ball accordingly.

## REPLANTING AZALEAS

Be sure to set the plant no deeper in the soil than its previous level, taking into account a centimetre or two of leafy or fibrous lime-free compost mulch which is best added later. If replanting in clayey soils, that is, any soil that becomes sticky when wet, then set the plant with its root mat slightly above soil level and build up to it and 1–2 cm (½ in) over it with a mixture of about half coarse sand or sandy soil and rotted leaf mould or moistened peat moss. In other words, azaleas hate clay above or washing into their roots but can be grown successfully on clay.

Do not apply fertiliser when replanting as this can harm the delicate root structure.

# ROSES — RESTORING THEIR GLORY

*I nvariably roses will reward the time spent on a revival, because their root system is quite resilient. You could well discover a once-fashionable, perfumed beauty in your favourite colour just waiting to bloom again, given the chance.*

In old neglected gardens you may uncover the remnants of rose bushes still clinging to life but sadly deteriorated because of heavy competition for light, moisture and nutrients by uncontrolled shrubbery, other growth, or rose scale. It may seem futile but there can be satisfaction as well as interest in reviving these game survivors.

The resuscitation technique depends on the time of year. During the warmer months, it is safest just to prune back overhanging growth, also dead canes or stems on the bush. Then give a prolonged but gentle soaking if the soil is dry, allowing the hose to just trickle around the base of the stem to make sure moisture penetrates to the roots. When the soil dries to just damp (this may take a day or two), break up the surface to the depth of 4 or 5 cm (2 in) and knead in a little compost or leaf mould. After a few weeks during warm conditions, signs of new growth should be apparent.

During winter, when growth is relatively dormant, after cleaning away dead growth as suggested above, prune any live stems back to the main structure of the plant. If you have decided to move the rose to a more favourable position, now is the time, preferably immediately after pruning.

Note that most roses are budded on to strong-rooted briar canes. The point where this budding has taken is usually woody and bulbous, sometimes at or a little below ground level. Particularly when bushes are neglected, the briar root-stock begins shooting and eventually takes over. The canes of the original rose die out. Check that newer canes do not come from below the bud union and, if so, cut off cleanly against the root-stem using a sharp pruning saw.

RIGHT: *A sunny cottage style garden is not complete without the addition of fragrant roses such as 'Mary Rose'. Classified as an English rose, this beauty, along with many others, has been bred to repeat-flower over a long season and to infuse an old world charm with their attractive, bushy growth.*

OPPOSITE: *'Dorothy Perkins', a favourite for many years, seen growing as a specimen lawn standard. After their late-spring flowering, the long stems can be somewhat reduced to make mowing during the sumer months easier.*

74

ABOVE: *Roses blend with a myriad of landscape styles. Here an old-fashioned climber is at home rambling over a rustic pergola while other roses prefer a sunny position in an open garden.*

ABOVE RIGHT: *Whether picking for the vase or deadheading, always endeavour to cut just above a leaf union to allow a dormant flowering shoot to emerge.*

Rose scale will debilitate and can eventually kill a rose bush. It appears as a white dandruff-like flecking or streaking mainly on older canes. Heavy infestation may form a white crusting, even on new canes, and appears mainly towards their base. Badly affected stems will need to be pruned and destroyed, then, if plants are dormant, sprayed with lime sulphur solution or white oil. This spray will burn new growth, so if the rose is to be treated in the growing season, paint stems only with the solution and spray foliage with a much more diluted solution, say 10 ml to a litre (or 1 fl oz to 6 pints) of water. Some products contain an oil base and can be used throughout the year (check the label before use).

### TRANSPLANTING AN OLD ROSE

Roses need a position that has at least half sun, preferably more, and is fairly open to provide good air circulation. They are best moved while dormant. A few weeks before the move, dig over the new site to about spade depth, at a time when the soil is just damp and has lost its stickiness. In cold, wet winter areas, this is best done in late autumn. A layer of compost decomposed almost to a soil-like condition may be mixed in with the soil at the same time but do not add fertiliser. Garden lime or dolomite may also be added, spreading up to two-thirds of a cup of either per square metre (3 ft square), particularly if the soil is known to be acid.

The soil may be left in its roughly dug state to aerate, then prior to the move, break up large clods and consolidate by treading it over,

### TESTING FOR ACIDITY

*A rough guide to acidity is that untreated hydrangeas are usually blue in acid soil and pink in alkaline or limey soils. There are relatively cheap and easy-to-use soil-testing kits available to check this.*

providing the soil is only just damp — not sticky.

Lift the old rose by spading down to full depth all around the plant, about 20 cm (8 in) out from the base — when the soil is damp but not sticky. This should cut main roots. Then go around the same cut again levering upwards, which should be enough to allow it to be lifted out. If not, trench around on the outside of the cut so that you can work under the plant — the soil ball may be held by an unusually large root or roots from surrounding trees or shrubs may be entangled and holding it fast.

Trim all roots with sharp, sterilised secateurs, then cover to prevent drying out while the new hole is being prepared, now that the size of the root ball is known. This should be no deeper than to bring the rose to its previous depth but wide enough to take the full spread of the roots, or if soil is still intact around them, about twice the width of the soil ball so that soil can be well-firmed in around it. Rake surplus soil in a ridge to make a water-holding saucer-like depression around the plant. Before filling this with water, it is a good idea to spread a layer of leaf mould, dead grass or other fibrous material as a buffer, so that the water does not puddle the soil surface and cause caking.

Do not feed for two to three months after new spring growth commences.

## REPLACING OLD ROSES

It is not wise to plant a new rose or transplant an old rose where another has been growing, as soil-borne organisms invariably cause what is known as 'rose sickness' in the newcomer. However, this can be overcome by removing as much of the old root as possible plus at least half a barrow of the soil, which should then be replaced with soil from another part of the garden where roses are not growing. This can be mixed with friable compost.

BELOW LEFT: *When space is at a premimum, why not include a bi-colour rose such as 'Chivilary' to give extra interest on the one bush.*

BELOW: *There is something special about red roses such as 'Riverview', and what is more rewarding than a bunch picked from your own bushes?*

# RECLAIMING FRUIT TREES

F ruit trees, especially old garden favourites such as apple, pear and plum trees, are easily reclaimed by the keen gardener who appreciates the value of fresh fruit. Revitalising is simple and always rewarding.

Apples, pears and most other fruit trees are attractive in growth and need not be relegated to the utility part of the garden as was once the custom. However, as with many ornamental trees, they do succumb to neglect.

If old apple trees are straggly with dead twiggy growth and tiny fruit, it could be due to pests or disease, or simply through competition for light, water and plant food, so easily forgotten as gardens and trees mature.

First check the bark of the tree for canker, or for any other sign of disease. Canker is a fungal disease which enters the tree through lesions on the trunk and branches. It first appears as a sunken patch and then as an open wound. Severely cankered trees should be grubbed out as the fungus is highly contagious and liable to infect other, healthy apple trees.

When the trunk and main branches of the apple tree seem reasonably sound, it is worth trying to rejuvenate the tree. This is best done in the winter when the tree is dormant. The first step is the removal of all dead and diseased wood, as well as the old twiggy branches, the banches which cross and rub each other or those that are inward growing. The branches should be removed cleanly, flush with the trunk. If the tree is too tall, cut the topmost branches back to lower ones, allowing light and air to penetrate through to the lower canopy. If the required pruning will remove half the total growth of the tree, spread the process out over two or three seasons.

Neglected apple trees which were trained in the past and have now grown away from their

RIGHT: *The mouthwatering fruit and striking colour offered by plum trees make them well worth saving.*

OPPOSITE: *An established Apple 'Fiesta' in blossom. After a little pruning and re-shaping, it provides a wonderful display along with the spring bulbs. Fruit trees need not be relegated to the rear of a garden when you can savour the sweet blossom plus the fruit close to outdoor living areas or ideally beside a path.*

supports will require different treatment. The regenerating pruning will need to be spread out over a period of several years. It may be more advisable to grub out the trees completely and start afresh.

Remove grass and weeds from around the base of your fruit tree. If deep-rooted weeds like couch or dock are present, suitable chemical sprays may be used, providing care is taken to shield the tree and avoid run-off.

A surface mulch of compost will be helpful when weeds have died, plus a generous amount of well-rotted manure and a top dressing of sulphate of potash.

Give the area a long but gentle soaking so that moisture penetrates to the subsoil. In fact, if other neglected trees are in the vicinity, it is wise to water and feed as wide an area as

ABOVE: *Figs may look a little stark in winter but their bold, dramatic leaves during the warmer months and delicious fruit in early autumn make them very worthwhile.*

RIGHT: *In cooler areas, the Spanish chestnut,* Castanea sativa, *provides summer shade as the tree matures and the bounty of an edible crop. The nuts, encased within spiny husks, fall on ripening, making harvesting a joy for both young and old. They should be gathered, using gloves, as soon as possible.*

possible to minimise root competition slowing the rejuvenation process.

When the tree responds to this attention, it will produce new shoots, mainly from behind the tip of each branch — usually too many. Select the two or three pointing in the direction where new well-spaced branches are desirable. It is better to select shoots slightly to the side of the branch as these tend to form more lateral, and therefore more crop-producing, growth than erect shoots.

Neglected pear trees can receive the same treatment as apple trees.

Plums and damsons will also need their growth thinning out. Remove the more upright branches and aim to keep growth more lateral.

Neglected peaches will normally need heavier pruning. Again, aim to encourage lateral growth and remove erect branches as close as possible to their base.

Old and neglected fig trees that have grown away from their supports should be severely pruned. They will throw out new shoots from the stumps, which can then be re-tied back to the wall or support.

Mulberry trees tend to grow to a fantastic age and will require little attention. Simply remove any dead branches.

ABOVE LEFT: *Pears, another easily grown garden plant with a delicious edible crop.*

ABOVE: *One of the joys of a home orchard is a fresh apple.*

# HERBACEOUS BORDERS FOR COTTAGE GARDENS

*C*ombinations of herbaceous and evergreen perennials, annuals and perhaps an occasional small shrub will provide fabulous seasonal colour and a pleasantly permanent appearance throughout the year.

Nearly all herbaceous plants go into dormancy and die down during winter, leaving the ground bare for four to six months. Therefore a more acceptable compromise, in particular for relatively small gardens, is a well-balanced combination of both evergreen and herbaceous perennials. Small- to medium-sized flowering or attractive foliaged plants also fit this cottage garden style mixture, and add permanence as well as variety.

There is no reason why drifts of annuals should not accompany the perennials to contribute seasonal colour. In fact, most of the herbaceous perennials do not flower until late spring and early summer, therefore annuals like Iceland poppies, stocks, linaria, larkspur and clumps of dwarf sweet peas can fill in during late winter and spring. Similarly, late-sown asters, bedding dahlias, petunias or torenia help carry the colour through until late autumn.

There are a number of long-flowering evergreen shrub-like perennials growing to about 1 m (3 ft) high and nearly as wide that are ideal for planting in a sun-drenched border between established shrubs. These include the range of double and single white, pink or yellow marguerites, the pink or white *Dimorphotheca* or

*Osteospermum* species, French lavender and slightly smaller blue kingfisher daisies that, with a light trim back after each flowering flush, will give colour for most of the year.

Geraniums, or more correctly Zonal pelargoniums, are invaluable contributors because they flower from spring right through to autumn. The fancy-leafed Zonal pelargoniums are at their best during winter but are still attractive during the warmer months. Several varieties, like 'Ann Tilling', have a soft lemon to lime colour during summer then deepen to gold with a reddish bronze zone through the leaf during colder months. These combine well with contrasting dark varieties like 'Leonie Holborow' which changes from bronze green to dark chocolate during winter.

These and hundreds of other pelargoniums in this category grow happily outdoors in all but very frosty and extreme tropical districts, and flower best with plenty of sun. If you live in a region prone to frost, keep the more tender pelargoniums under glass until the frosts have passed, using them then as summer bedding. (Alternatively, look for the many attractive and scented true geraniums that will thrive in cooler conditions.) Keep growth compact by pinching tips from new shoots when they reach about finger length.

OPPOSITE: *Cottage gardening is very rewarding especially when the chosen plants meld together in a harmonious flow of colour. Part of the joy of this form of gardening is arranging pleasing combinations and the fact that they can be changed next season. Perennials are easily moved, or divided to increase stock, making revision a low-cost gardening delight.*

**Key**

1. *Escallonia macrantha* 'Rosea'
2. *Hibiscus syriacus* 'Oiseau Blue'
3. *Grevillea* 'Honey Gem'
4. *Camellia sasanqua* 'Plantation Pink'
5. Butterfly bush (*Buddleia davidii*)
6. Syrian hibiscus (*Hibiscus syriacus*)
7. Mauve bottlebrush (*Callistemon citrinus* 'Burgundy')
8. *Escallonia macrantha* 'Apple Blossom'
9. *Spiraea thunbergii*
10. Lavender (*Lavandula dentata*)

5.

6.

7.

8.

9.

## SHRUB AND PERENNIAL BORDER IN MID SUMMER

A single line border planting of shrubs has been widened and shaped to allow for colourful perennial plants to be used, grading down from the spires of hollyhocks, delphiniums and foxgloves to edging plants such as the dianthus, giant ajuga and Swan River daisy. Among the additions in the renovation are three Spirea thunbergii, a medium-sized shrub with feathery foliage, limey green through summer, turning gold and then shades of bronze in autumn, briefly showing bare wiry stems in winter, soon dotted with tiny white single star flowers persisting among the spring foliage.

# Dividing Perennials

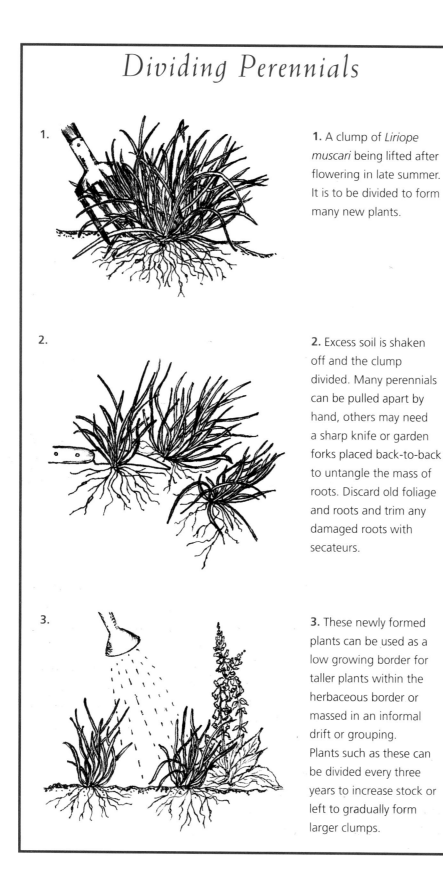

**1.** A clump of *Liriope muscari* being lifted after flowering in late summer. It is to be divided to form many new plants.

**2.** Excess soil is shaken off and the clump divided. Many perennials can be pulled apart by hand, others may need a sharp knife or garden forks placed back-to-back to untangle the mass of roots. Discard old foliage and roots and trim any damaged roots with secateurs.

**3.** These newly formed plants can be used as a low growing border for taller plants within the herbaceous border or massed in an informal drift or grouping. Plants such as these can be divided every three years to increase stock or left to gradually form larger clumps.

Those grown for flower display are pruned progressively from late-summer as each stem stops producing flower buds, and coloured leaf types are usually left until spring. Bearded irises are wonderful value in cottage gardens. Their evergreen upright blue-grey foliage adds a pleasing form amongst undulating growth, and the mid to late spring flowers are superb. Keep them towards the foreground as overshadowing by taller plants can reduce the flower spike numbers.

There are also the taller Louisiana and Spuria hybrids which reach one metre (3 ft) or more, have spectacular flowers usually a little later than Bearded hybrids, but their growth is usually less permanent. Louisiana irises suit a slightly acid soil, whereas Bearded hybrids prefer a more alkaline situation.

Countless evergreens will keep the foreground of the garden well-covered. Many are long-flowering. Some, like white perennial Candytuft, the many Dianthus, including the clove-scented pinks and Swan River daisies, make low clumpy mounds. Others, including alpine phlox, that revel in the cooler temperate districts, arabis, ajuga, arenaria and Snow-in-summer (*Cerastium tomentosum*) are carpeters or trailers.

If the garden is sunny, a few roses can add immeasurably to the atmosphere, provided that they will not be crowded by other plants. Varieties like 'Iceberg' are long-flowering and pleasantly tall, very suitable for backgrounds. Climbing roses, especially 'Titian', a strong-growing, free-flowering rosy red, are also excellent backgrounds where they can be trained up walls or fences. Low-growing and compact cluster varieties like pink-flowered 'The Fairy' make showy foreground specimens. Don't overlook some of the old-fashioned or heritage roses now freely available, or the more modern David Austin varieties, as these help to create the old cottage garden atmosphere.

Most herbaceous perennials are now available as potted plants in flower as well as in mixed punnets. Otherwise they are normally planted from division of roots or more usually from outer suckers of clumps during late winter to early spring just as growth is starting. When planting in mixed beds, always mark the clumps at least with one or two pegs, and preferably with some form of label. Unlabelled clumps are likely to be destroyed when dormant by cultivation, or overplanted with later additions to the garden. This also applies to bulbs, which are easily 'lost' when the foliage dies down.

When buying herbaceous perennials, check flowering time so you can plan some colour continuity and combinations. For example, the different shasta daisies flower mainly in late spring to early summer, perennial phlox usually following on from then until autumn. Perennial asters, sometimes called Easter or Michaelmas daisies, vary a little with the variety – some may begin in early summer (depending on area) while some varieties may be a month later. *Lythrum virgatum* displays its spires of rosy pink flowers from early summer to autumn and is happy in well-drained or soggy soils. Some other daisies, like the golden *Helianthus salicifolius* and *Rudbeckia laciniata* 'Golden Glow', are at their peak in early to mid-autumn, whereas Stoke's aster (*Stokesia laevis*) carries lavender blue flowers in bursts from late spring to mid-autumn.

Check also on growth type, because the effect is more interesting if the usually rounded or undulating form is relieved here and there by clumps of others with tall spire-like form. The latter include long-flowering rosy-pink *Lythrum virgatum* which with reasonable moisture may reach 1.75 m (5½ ft), hollyhocks (2–2.5 m [6–8 ft]), foxgloves (1–1.5 m [3–5 ft]), perennial asters (to about 1 m [3 ft]), perennial blue salvia (*S. farinacea*; about 0.75 m [2½ ft]), lupins (in cool climates, to 1.5 m [5 ft]) and delphiniums (often treated as annuals in warm climates, to 2 m [6 ft]).

Another idea that adds a pleasant and natural appearance to perennial borders or areas where space is available, is to introduce a few annuals or biennials that resow themselves easily, if allowed to remain long enough to drop seeds. Amongst these are sky-blue *Anchusa capensis*, love-in-the-mist (*Nigella damascena*), linaria, viscaria, Californian, Shirley or Flanders poppy and *Viola tricolor*. Honesty seed can be scattered when its moon-like silvery white discs are peeled after the pods mature.

Primulas also reseed freely in shaded and not-too-dry positions. Just thin out or transplant excess seedlings before they overcrowd their neighbours.

ABOVE: *There's something about cosmos that evokes a feeling of wellbeing. Perhaps it's because they are so easy to grow. Available in many colours, including a deep chocolate brown, they certainly give an instant cottage garden look to even the most neglected garden.*

# GROUND COVERS — THE ANSWER TO WEED CONTROL

**W**eeding between mixed perennials, shrubs or seedlings can be time-consuming. Some people find it relaxing, others frustrating. Ground covers, once well-established, can eliminate most of this routine and time-consuming maintenance.

Plants that hug the ground in a tight, weed-suppressing mat need not make the garden look static. It is possible to have patches of cover plants with different textures and colours. Clumps of bulbous plants can be successfully planted under or through the carpeting types, or height can be varied by combining some of the suggested prostrate or low-branching shrubs. Experiment with a few different varieties to determine which suits your particular conditions and taste. Be guided by the following lists, and, within a season or two, weeding will become a minor task in the garden calendar.

### ESTABLISHING GROUND COVERS
Before planting carpeting-type ground covers which are usually set 50 cm to 1 m (1½ to 3 ft) apart, it is a good idea to spread a 4–5 cm (1½–2 in) layer of leaf mould or woodchip to deter any further growth from dormant weed seeds. Rake back sufficient of this mulch to set each plant in, then return it to cover any bared soil, ensuring that the mulch just clears the stems of the newly planted ground cover.

Watering through the mulch rather than directly onto the soil will also speed development of root growth by preventing surface soil caking.

If the leaf mould or other organic mulch is decomposing and thinning out before the plants have made complete cover, then just apply more to these thin areas.

### CARPETING GROUND COVERS FOR DENSE OR LIGHT SHADE
Asarabacca (*Asarum europauem*) — Kidney-shaped leaves form an evergreen, ground-hugging cover in neutral to acid soil. The glossy leaves conceal small greenish-purple flowers in spring..

Australian violet (*Viola hederacea*) — 5–8 cm (2–3 in). Mat of bright green variable rounded to kidney-shaped foliage about 3 cm (1 in) across. Small violet-shaped flowers, usually palest mauve to white with violet throat, on erect 7–9 cm (2½–3½ in) stems. Usually flowers in flushes from mid-spring to early winter in all but dense shade.

Baby's tears or 'mind-your-own-business' (*Soleirolia soleirolii*) — Light green moss-like carpet of tiny rounded foliage, covers damp soil or rocks fairly rapidly.

Barren's wort (*Epimedium* x *rubrum*) — Heart shaped leaves, tinged red when young and again blushing red-brown in autumn. Bears

*OPPOSITE: Ivy, while smothering weeds, can also present its own problem if left unclipped too long or allowed to climb trees. However, it can be a good choice where it is easily contained in a bed surrounded by paving. Likewise, the fishbone fern can be invasive but is contained here under maturing tree ferns and . within the bounds of defined garden beds. In the open sunny areas of the garden, plants are being encouraged to spread and form a colourful lilac-blue mat.*

delicate crimson and yellow flowers in spring. Forms a low-growing mound up to 30 cm (12 in) high.

Bell flower (*Campanula poscharskyana*) — 10–15 cm (4–6 in) high. Carpet of mid-green foliage, massed with 20–25 cm (8–10 in) sprays of pale lavender blue flowers, mainly mid-spring. Later, when finished, these flower stems are easily cut or can be pulled away in handfuls. Plants spread readily in temperate or cool areas. Happy with about half-sun or light shade.

Dead nettle (*Lamium maculatum*) — Attractive clumps of 6–8 cm (2½–3in)-long oval silver-grey and dark green foliage, on wiry stems that by late spring are extending 50 cm to 1m (1½ to 3 ft) away to layer and form new clumps. Therefore it can travel rapidly. Suits shrubberies.

Ferns — Most types including maidenhair (*Adiantum* species) grow well in reasonably moist shade. Fishbone types (*Nephrolepis*) accept drier conditions and heavy root competition, especially *N. cordifolia*, sword fern. These ferns can be invasive. The Heart's Tongue fern (*Asplenium scolopendrium*) will grow in surprisingly dry areas, young seedlings often taking root at the foot of walls.

Florists violet (*Viola odorata*) — This violet (and its many hybrids) with its larger and darker green foliage than *V. hederacea* makes a dense and usually weed-free carpeter and, if shade is not too dense, will provide flowers during late winter and early spring.

Golden oregano (*Origanum vulgare* 'Aureum') — Dense growth of erect stems to 30 cm (12 in) like culinary oregano, (and similarly aromatic) leaves 2–3 cm (1 in) long but a deep golden colour except during the cold months. Best cut back in late winter. Colours best in full sun. Propagate by division or cuttings.

*Hosta* — Most types enjoy full shade, though yellow-leaved varieties colour better with some sun. Hostas are grown for their bold architectural leaves in varying shades of green. Unfortunately very prone to slug attack; dislikes drought.

Ivy (*Hedera helix*) — 'California fan' or 'Pittsburgh' hybrids make interesting cover but if not checked occasionally, may climb and become invasive.

Knotweed (*Persicaria capitata* syn. *Polygonum capitatum*) — Dull-green oval to pointed leaves about 6 cm (2½ in) long, turning reddish bronze in dry sunny positions. Erect spikes with pink clusters of flower heads resembling tiny strawberries in shape. Sometimes regarded as a weed but makes a tough and attractive cover for banks or rocky outcrops where weeding is difficult.

Lesser periwinkle (*Vinca minor*) — A prostrate evergreen shrub to 15 cm (6 in) high, with long trailing shoots and dark green leaves. Carries attractive rich violet flowers from summer to autumn. The Greater periwinkle is often invasive, but the variegated cultivar *Vinca major* 'Variegata' is attractive and well behaved.

Mondo grass (*Ophiopogon japonicus*) — Mat of dark, glossy green, fine tufted foliage to

*BELOW: A colourful plant, Hypericum x moserianum looks well when group-planted as a ground cover in the front of a shrub border. They flower best in a full sun position in cooler areas. Prune lightly after the summer-through-autumn flowers fade to remove seed heads and to promote a more compact cover. Like many other plants, these tips can be used to increase stock but success is more assured if cuttings are taken during the warmer months.*

LEFT: *There are many plants which will form a colourful dense mat over bare earth to inhibit the growth of weeds. Some are more vigorous than others and it pays to keep watch over an area to be sure that they don't smother others. A gentle hand, often applied in cutting back, will result in an ordered, yet relaxed-looking garden rather than a once-a-year clean-up that so often leaves an area once again open to weed growth.*

20 cm (8 in). Stands dryness and sun as well as complete shade.

*Pachysandra terminalis* — Coarsely toothed, glossy dark green leaves to 10 cm (4 in). Spreads easily, especially in moist humus rich soil. *P.t.* 'Variegata' is slower to spread, but has attractive white edged leaves.

Sweet woodruff (*Gallium odoratum*) — An attractive woodland perennial with fresh green leaves growing to 45 cm (18 in) tall. The white star-shaped flowers in the summer are scented and attractive to bees.

Wood anemone (*Anemone nemorosa*) — Low growing, to 15 cm (6 in), with fresh green, deeply divided leaves. In spring to early summer carries single white flowers.

## CARPETING GROUND COVERS FOR DAPPLED SHADE TO FULL SUN

Aurora daisy (*Arctotis* hybrids) — Low mass of divided silver-grey foliage, pink cream or bronze-zoned daisies on 15–20 cm (6–8 in) stems, mainly in spring to early summer. Withstands dryness when established, best in full sun.

Alpine phlox (*Phlox subulata*) — Dense mats of blue-green grass-like foliage hidden below a mass of starry deep or pale pink, rosy red, mauve or white flowers from early spring and sometimes carrying into summer. Best in cool districts but worth trying in all but hotter temperate districts with adequate watering, and light feeding every six weeks from early spring until summer. Needs at least half sun — in cool areas, flowers more profusely in full sun.

*Bergenia cordifolia* — Loose rosettes of large leathery green wedge-shaped leaves, and attractive sprays of pink waxy flowers in winter — early spring.

Bugle (*Ajuga reptans*) — Creates a carpet of bronze-green rosetted foliage, spikes to 20 cm (8 in) of blue flowers in spring; accepts wet to moderately dry soil.

Busy Lizzy (*Impatiens walleriana*) — The dwarf strains in particular (growing to about 20 cm [8 in]) are an excellent temporary ground cover, quick-growing and very colourful in sun or shade if soil is not excessively dry. They flower profusely throughout the warmer months until frost and are renewed easily from cuttings or seed. Older taller types are good 'fillers' for summer colour in shade but if not controlled will choke out smaller plants, as seeds are flung up to 2 m (6 ft) or more as pods explode and germinate rapidly. Also happy in the shade.

Chamomile (*Chamaemelum nobile*) — Light carpet of finely divided green foliage with small white daisy flowers borne in late spring or summer, used in cool to cooler temperate areas as lawn. The best variety for lawns is the non-flowering form, 'Treneague'. Not entirely weed-proof; withstands some foot traffic. Flowers can also be used to make tea.

*Convolvulus sabatius* (syn *C. mauritanicus*) trails to about 1m (3 ft) long, soft-green foliage and lavender-blue saucer shaped flowers 2–2.5 cm (1 in) across open during sunlight in summer and early autumn.

Common sage (*Salvia officinalis*) — For a position in full sun, sage offers a culinary delight as well as a feast to the eye with its wooly, aromatic, grey leaves. For a dash of colour, try *S. o.* 'Tricolor', as the soft leaves of this herb are splashed with pink. The leaves of *S. o.* 'Purpurescens' are a red-purple colour.

Cotton lavender (*Santolina pinnata neapolitana*) — For well drained soil in the sun, this plant has grey-green aromatic leaves and bears a profusion of bright yellow button flower heads in the summer. It is also a suitable plant for low hedging.

Creeping phlox (*Phlox stolonifera*) — Herbaceous perennial up to 10 cm (4 in) high. Bears pale to rich purple flowers in the early summer. *P. s.* 'Ariane' has paler leaves and white flowers.

Dog's fennel (*Anthemis tinctoria*) — Dense mat of fine dark-green foliage, robust bright golden daisies on 30–40 cm (12–16 in) stems, mostly in early summer. Showy foreground plant or soil binder in half-sun or more. Pale yellow cultivars are available.

Gazania cultivars — Mats of leathery foliage, displaying bright daisies 5–7 cm (2–2½ in) across in cream, gold orange-bronze and burgundy, usually with darker centre zone. Best in full sun — accepts sea coast conditions.

*Lithodora diffusa* 'Heavenly Blue' — Growing to 15 cm (6 in), this evergreen shrub thrives on acid humus rich soils. Produces a wealth of deep blue flowers in the spring and summer.

Money wort (*Lysimachia nummularia*) — Ground or rock-hugging carpet of rounded dark-green foliage on wandering stems which take root easily. Occasionally studded in spring with stemless flowers like buttercups. A golden form 'Aurea' is also available. Suits moist soil.

Sandwort (*Arenaria montana*) — Fine-leafed carpeter or trailer with small, glistening white saucer-shaped flowers in summer. Must have adequate moisture.

*Saxifraga stolonifera* or Mother of thousands — Trailer with rosettes of lighter-veined, rounded, dull green or variegated leaves. Tiny sprays of whitish flowers, form red thread-like stolons to 30 cm (12 in) or so long, carrying plantlets. Suits shaded areas — not particularly weed-inhibiting in damp light shade.

LEFT: *Rather than allowing the garden to meet with the lawn on level ground, the garden behind the wall was back-filled with good soil in which a well-ordered collection of low-growing plants can be easily tendered from the lawn area. Note how plants graduate in height to tie in with the trees behind and how a mower strip allows plants to tumble unimpeded over the wall.*

BELOW: *Stepping stones entice the viewer into the seemingly wild garden while allowing the fallen nuts of the macadamia tree, top left, to be easily collected. Note how a collection of white flowering and grey foliage plants in the foreground help to give depth.*

*Saxifraga* x *urbium* — One of about 300 species, sometimes also known as London pride. In cool districts, makes an attractive spring cloud-like display of pale pink or white tiny flowers, on fine stems about 15 cm (6 in) above clumps of thick oval to oblong leaves 5–6 cm (2 in) long.

Seaside daisy (*Erigeron karvinskianus*) — Quick-growing mounds of stems with small divided foliage, almost covered for most of the year with very fine petalled, white-flushed pink daisies about 1.7 cm (½ in) across on thread-like stems. Reseeds freely and perhaps a little invasive but a wonderful cover for banks or walls.

Snow-in-summer (*Cerastium tomentosum*) — Carpet of silver-grey foliage, covered with small white saucer shaped flowers in late spring.

Swan River daisy (*Brachyscome iberidifolia*) — Net-like mats of very finely divided, bright green foliage with fine-petalled lilac flowers about 2 cm (½ in) across from spring into autumn — spreads 30–50 cm (12–20 in).

Thyme (*Thymus* species) — Usually used between stepping stones for aroma when brushed, but in cool climates, 'Westmoreland' especially is sometimes used as ground cover or lawn. Needs open position with at least half-sun. In very hot, dry climates use wild thyme (*Thymus serpyllum*); in early summer this has the advantage of masses of mauve, purple, white or pink flowers.

## PLANTS WHICH DEMAND SUN FOR AT LEAST HALF THE DAY

This group also contains low-branching shrub-like long flowering woody perennials such as marguerite daisies and lavenders, already mentioned in the section on cottage gardens p 82, which make good ground covers when mass-planted. All are improved by pruning after flowering, are easily grown from cuttings, and develop compact growth and kept bushy by pinching back or tip-pruning back; finger-length shoots as growth progresses.

### PROSTRATE WOODY SHRUBS

Creeping juniper (*Juniperus horizontalis*) — Attractive ground-hugging plants with densely packed feather like 'plumes' or branchlets of foliage. Many cultivars of this species are available, including 'Douglasii' with ground-hugging branches bearing slightly ascending greyish-green foliage to about 45 cm (17½ in) and spreading 1.5 m (5 ft). Some cultivars have foliage that changes to purplish hues in winter. Average height from 25–30 cm (10–16 in) high in 10 years with a spread of 2–3 m (6–9 ft). Some increase as much as 30–40 cm (12–16 in) in a year — space about 1.5 m (5 ft) apart but check colour and habit with your local nursery.

*J. sabina* 'Tamariscifolia' — An attractive green juniper with soft ascending growth from horizontal branches, usually reaching about 50 cm (1½ ft) high and 1.5 m (5 ft) wide.

*J. communis* 'Depressa Aurea' — Horizontal branches with pendulous tip growth, grey-blue in summer, light bronze in autumn, stately purple in late winter with golden tip growth in spring. Reaches about 30 cm (12 in) high and little more than 2 m (6 ft) wide in 10 years.

Kohuhu (*Pittosporum tenuifolium* 'Tom Thumb') — Growing to 1 m (3 ft) tall, this slow growing shrub bears shiny, spoon-shaped foliage, flushed an agreeable purple.

*Leptospermum rupestre* — A relative of the tea tree, this low-growing, evergreen shrub has glossy, deep green aromatic leaves. White, star-shaped flowers are borne in the summer.

Rock Rose (*Helianthemum* species) — Evergreen shrubs ideal for rock gardens or sunny borders. The many named hybrids offer a wide range of flower colour. However, they are short lived and need frequent replacing.

### CLIMBERS AS GROUND COVERS

The following climbing plants also make suitable ground covers. They can be encouraged to branch to make denser cover or curtailed, if wandering too far, by redirecting or pruning back runners.

*Clematis armandii* — growing in full sun or shade this evergreen climber does require some frost protection. If the conditions are suitable it will soon be scrambling over the bank, bursting into scented flower in spring. This is an ideal manner in which to grow this clematis because often, as when scrambling up a tree, the flowers are out of sight and impossible to smell.

*Hydrangea anomala* ssp *petiolaris* — This self-clinging climber can reach heights of 20 m (65 ft), even in dark and shady corners. During the summer, creamy white flowers are borne freely above the deciduous leaves. Although slow to start, this climber will happily cover a sun-starved bank in the shade.

Potato Vine (*Solanum crispum*) — A rambling creeper that will advance happily along the ground. The cultivar 'Glasnevin' has gorgeous mauve blue flowers throughout the summer.

Star jasmine (*Trachelospermum jasminoides*) — Normally grown as a climber or trailer, but will eventually self-layer in the garden and, if ends are clipped back occasionally, will form a glossy dark-green mat spangled with starry creamy white and very aromatic flowers in late spring and early summer. The cultivar 'Variegatum' has new shoots soft pink at the tip, white below, then dark-green speckled white and maturing to an even dark-green, but it rarely flowers.

*Trachelospermum asiaticum* has duller and stiffer deep-green foliage than *T. jasminoides*, with less significant, tubular, creamy-yellowish flowers. However, it is considered hardier and more adaptable. Prefers a well drained soil and will grow in sun or semi-shade.

## ERECT OR SEMI-ERECT EVERGREEN BULBOUS PLANT

These plants give variety of form amongst carpeting ground cover.

*Agapanthus praecox*, subsp. *orientalis* — This is the most popular species. Forms dense clumps 75 cm to 1 m (2 to 3 ft) high, bright-green strap-like foliage — tall spikes with large heads of blue or white flowers from early to midsummer or later. Tough competitive and soil-binding roots. Needs up to half-sun to flower well. Dwarf varieties also available.

Day lilies (*Hemerocallis*) — Evergreen hybrids are now available to ensure year-round interest and weed-free coverage. Their arching green, strap-like foliage is densely packed, forming clumps about 50 cm to 1 m (1½ to 3 ft) wide. Above these the cream, gold, orange burgundy, rosy mauve or purple trumpet-shaped flowers appear from late spring to midsummer. Best with at least half-sun.

*Dierama pulcherrimum* (Angels' fishing rod, Wand flower) — During the summer produces arching stems of pink bell-like flowers. These are held high and above the thin, grass-like leaves. Enjoys well-drained soil in full sun and is most effective when situated overhanging a stream or pond.

*Imperata cylindrica* 'Rubra' — Although slow to spread, this wonderful slender grass more than earns its keep with its colourful display. The flat, mid-green leaves up to 40 cm (16 in) tall, quickly turn a dramatic blood red from their very tips almost to the base. Will suit full sun or dappled shade. Looks particularly dramatic against a dark backdrop.

*Libertia formosa* — Stiff, iris-like, evergreen

leaves form an excellent contrast to low-growing horizontal lines. Bears small, white or pale yellow flowers in the early summer. In areas prone to frost it may require some protection in the form of a dry winter mulch.

Lily turf (*Ophiopogon planiscapus* 'Nigrescens') — A popular choice among garden designers, this low-growing plant, up to 20 cm (8 in) tall, provides unusual colour contrast for many shrubs and low-growing ground cover. Strap-shaped, almost black leaves, to 30 cm (12 in) long, grow in an almost spider-like formation.

Ribbon grass (*Liriope muscari*) — The variegated form makes attractive dense clumps of tough, slender, strap-like foliage 30–35 cm (12–14 in) high with spikes of violet blue flowers in late summer to autumn. Well-suited for use as an accent amongst lower carpeting cover. Accepts root competition; sun or light shade.

ABOVE: *Over recent years, many new hybrid day lilies in a wide and intriguing colour range have become available. They look particularly good when mass-planted if one colour only is chosen, but are equally adaptable to be spot-planted in amongst the foreground shrubs. Evergreen, these new hybrids still retain the habit of producing only day-long flowers but as they are freely produced, it doesn't appear to matter.*

# CLIMBERS TO ADD THE FINISHING TOUCH

*C*limbers are among the most useful of plants. Given the right support, they will add a subtle elegance to the restoration of a garden.

Climbers are not static growers like other plants; they can trail for metres providing colour where it is needed regardless of whether there's soil directly available. They can climb into an impossibly tight spot in the garden as they take up vertical air space rather than valuable ground area; they can scramble up to a first floor balcony to act as a shade or privacy barrier, or just drape their magnificent blooms.

Most climbers need some kind of support onto which they can be trained. This support is indicative of the type of vine that is best selected. They attach themselves by various means, some have tendrils which twine around fine supports like wire, others have hooks, which in their natural habitat are used to hitch the long limp branches up to the sunlight, while others have aerial roots or suckers which can cling onto a hard surface such as a masonry wall with no other support needed. There's vigorous and dainty climbers and some, as mentioned on p 94, that are quite happy to suppress weeds when used as ground covers.

However, for all their other attributes, it is their ability to shade outdoor eating areas during the heat of summer that endears them to gardeners. Select a deciduous vine and you'll get the bonus of winter sun.

To gain the most from a climbing plant it must have a suitable frame on which to grow. No good giving a robust and strong vine a less-than-sturdy frame on which to support it. Many

RIGHT: *Climbing plants bring a graceful quality to the garden. Here, a rose arbour has been created to divide a large garden. For many weeks during spring, the stunning spectacle of 'Cottage Pink' in bloom is the focal point of the entire garden.*

OPPOSITE: *When space is tight and paving leads right up to a wall, then a combination of pots and climbers is the obvious answer. With the addition of lattice and potted colour, the scene is considerably enhanced.*

# Climbing Plants

D = deciduous        E = evergreen       C = for cool to cool temperate

S = needs some support    * = covers rapidly    L = self layering

| Common name | Botanical name | Details | Code |
|---|---|---|---|
| | *Actinidia kolomikta* | green, variegated leaves tinged white and pink, white flowers in summer | D |
| Bittersweet | *Celastrus scandens* | tiny, greenish flowers are borne in small clusters; also produces spherical fruits in bunches | D |
| Boston ivy | *Parthenocissus tricuspidata* | vigorous climber with spectacular crimson autumn colour | *D |
| Chinese trumpet creeper | *Campsis grandiflora* | masses of scarlet-orange tubular flowers | DL |
| Chocolate vine | *Akebia quinata* | purple-brown flowers amid interesting leaves | *DL |
| Climbing hydrangea | *Hydrangea petiolaris* | self-clinging; attractive, lacy clusters of white flowers | D |
| Japanese hydrangea | *Schizophragma hydrangeoides* | self-clinging, slightly fragrant white flowers | D |
| Common jasmine | *Jasminum officinale* | a neat, shrubby climber with fragrant white flowers | S |
| Clematis: | | | |
| | *Clematis armandii* | strong-growing, early-flowering, scented white flowers | *E |
| | *C. macropetala* | semi-double mauve-blue flowers | DC |
| | *C. montana* | vigorous, bares masses of pale pink single blossoms in spring | DC |
| | *C. 'Jackmanii'* | vigorous, velvety, dark purple flowers, fading to violet | D |
| | *C. 'Nelly Moser'* | large, rose-mauve flowers with a carmine stripe on each petal that fades in strong sun | D |
| | *C. 'Star of India'* | large plum-red flowers | E |
| Flame Creeper | *Tropaeolum speciosum* | scarlet flowers in summer, followed by bright blue fruits | |
| Grape vine | *Vitis vinifera* | excellent coverage for pergola plus fruit | *DS |
| Honey suckle | *Lonicera japonica* 'Halliana' | graceful climber with highly fragrant white and yellow flowers | *S |
| Hop | *Humulus lupulus* 'Aureus' | golden yellow foliage; excellent trained over a fence or trellis | D |
| | *Jasminum polyanthum* | strongly perfumed spring blossoms | *EL |
| Passionflower | *Passiflora caerulea* | fast-growing tendril climber with unique, showy flowers | *ES |
| | *Pileostegia viburnoides* | creamy white flowers borne in late summer | E |
| Potato vine | *Solanum jasminoides* | quick-growing with pale blue or white flowers in summer | *ES |
| Roses: | | | |
| | *Rosa* 'Blush Rambler' | vigorous scrambler, particularly good for arches and pergolas, with light pink flowers | *S |
| | *R.* 'Madame Alfred Carrière' | noisette climber, fragrant double flowers are creamy-white | S |
| | *R.* Rambling Rector' | rampant rambler, with clusters of scented creamy-white flowers | *S |
| | *R.* 'Veilchenblau' | vigorous rambler, rosette, double, violet flowers streaked white | *S |

# Climbing Plants

D = deciduous          E = evergreen          C = for cool to cool temperate
S = needs some support     * = covers rapidly     L = self layering

| Common name | Botanical name | Details | Code |
|---|---|---|---|
| Russian vine | *Fallopia baldschuanica* | also called 'mile-a-minute plant'; produces drooping panicles of pink or white flowers | *D |
| | *Solanum crispum* 'Glasnevin' | vigorous scrambler, clusters of lilac to purple flowers | E |
| Star jasmine | *Trachelospermum jasminoides* | provides a dense green cover with very fragrant, white summer flowers | E |
| Sweet pea | *Lathyrus odoratus* | fast-growing tendril climber with fragrant, attractive flowers | *S |
| Trumpet vine | *Campsis radicans* | orange, scarlet or yellow flowers | DL |
| Virginia creeper | *Parthenocissus quinquefolia* | robust, self-clinging vine with striking red autumn colour; gives good coverage | *D |
| | *Vitis coignetiae* | ornamental vine with good red autumn colour | |
| Wisteria: | *Wisteria floribunda* W. sinensis | produces stunning, long racemes of scented, lilac flowers; the woody framework of branches look good architecturally | DS DS |

LEFT: *There is a climber suited to every climate and one of the most popular combinations is a partnership of climbing roses and clematis. Here,* Rosa *'Raymond Chenault' and* Clematis *'Perle d'Azur' make a striking colour statement.*

# Dividing with Style

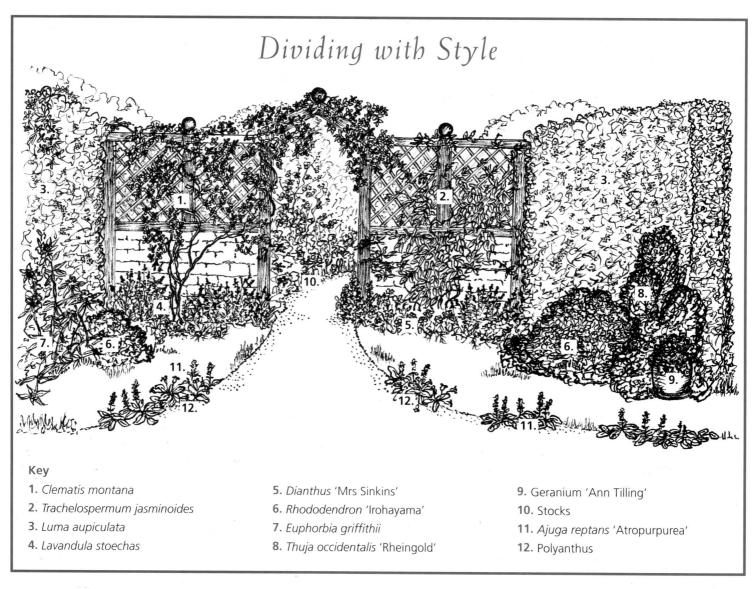

**Key**

1. *Clematis montana*
2. *Trachelospermum jasminoides*
3. *Luma aupiculata*
4. *Lavandula stoechas*

5. *Dianthus* 'Mrs Sinkins'
6. *Rhododendron* 'Irohayama'
7. *Euphorbia griffithii*
8. *Thuja occidentalis* 'Rheingold'

9. Geranium 'Ann Tilling'
10. Stocks
11. *Ajuga reptans* 'Atropurpurea'
12. Polyanthus

ABOVE: *Dividing a garden can provide many practical purposes so why not separate in style while providing a perfect position for some favourite climbing plants.*

established gardens incorporate a pergola as sun protection. However, there are now some wonderful ready-made gazebos or summer house designs available to incorporate into the garden makeover. These can provide a shady spot in which to sit and survey the garden, as well as being an enticing focal point when viewed from within the house. These structures are often the perfect place on which to display a favourite climbing plant.

As a vine such as a wisteria matures, the main trunk can become almost as thick as a tree trunk as it twists its way up a supporting pole.

If you find yourself confronted with such a plant, and the supporting structure is unsound, it is possible to hard-prune to turn the plant into a self-supporting standard about 1.3 m (4 ft) high or higher, with the aid of a metal stake. Also, rather than discarding a plant as well as the decaying structure, many climbers can be cut almost to the ground to enable the supporting structure to be rebuilt, then strong, new shoots can be selected and trained up the new structure maybe with the addition of some wire supports.

Generally though, climbers can be pruned

very much like shrubs. If multiple stems are required for an espaliered effect, then tip-pruning will encourage a single stem to become branched. If you want to encourage the plant to quickly reach a certain height before branching, side shoots can be rubbed off until the required height is reached. Likewise, most vines can be cut back after flowering to keep them in check but it is more rewarding to select the right vine for a particular position.

A limited space against a wall is soon filled and a vigorous climber may need to be cut back at regular intervals so that it rarely has a chance to flower. However, a more slender vine could give you a continuous display throughout the season.

If existing paving precludes planting, vines are easily grown in containers at the base of a pergola. In fact, by planting a climber in a large pot, the surface area can be filled with decorative annuals or other plants to tumble over the edges and provide a cool root run for the main plant. This is often a very necessary precaution in the heat of summer and provides a colourful addition during the winter months when the main vine may be dormant.

A substantial tub or container is needed to provide a climber with a viable root area, with the likelihood that it will remain *in situ* for many years. Consequently, it should be filled with the best possible potting mix to ensure continued healthy growth. In addition, regular light fertilising will speed plant growth and ensure the best possible blooms.

BELOW LEFT: Solanum jasminoides *'Album'* cools the heat of the walled garden with its elegant clusters of white flowers.

BELOW: Wisteria floribunda *'Macrobotrys'* complements the arched gateway in this courtyard.

# HEDGES AND WINDBREAKS — THE FENCE ALTERNATIVE

*N*eatly clipped hedges have, for many centuries, been the alternative to brick or masonry walls to create privacy, to introduce a formal atmosphere into the garden or to divide a large garden into sections.

Today's choice for privacy or a windbreak is more usually a row of small evergreen trees or shrubs chosen because they reach an appreciable height fairly rapidly, and hopefully will remain at the desired height. Realistically, there is nothing that grows rapidly to a specified height and retains that height or width naturally, but there are some plants with moderate growth rates that are fairly easy to keep at a reasonable height — they are listed on the following pages.

## WINDBREAKS

Erecting solid walls, high fences or planting dense hedges does not necessarily solve wind problems. The action of wind when it meets a solid or dense barrier is to jump it, then perhaps only a few metres (feet) further on, to curl downwards towards the ground before continuing forward. A less dense hedge, on the other hand, say with growth sparse enough to see through at close quarters, will filter the wind and reduce its force, usually to a more comfortable rate (see diagrams on p 107).

## REJUVENATING OLD HEDGES

When a once-formal hedge has been neglected for a long time and the original runaway growth has continued to branch, the best plan is to saw back all branches too heavy to trim, 25–30 cm (10–12 in) below the desired height.

Speed new growth by scattering a dressing of nitrogen-rich fertiliser such as lawn food a little out from the base of the hedge then give a good gentle soaking. Note that response will be best in spring, and minimal during cold conditions. When new growth reaches the desired height, trim back to about half to induce side shoots. From then on, it should be thick enough to trim periodically, bearing in mind it will be growing quickly with the fertiliser.

RIGHT: *Low box hedges provide a defining edge to both path and lawn area while helping to add a perspective of length to this section of the garden.*

OPPOSITE: *A sense of formality provided by the wide set of stairs is further enhanced by the clipped hedges on either side plus the neatly clipped balls, but this formal approach is offset by the curving trunk of the tree at the top of the wide flight of stairs.*

# Plants Suitable for Hedges

T = suitable for trimming          S = suitable for coastal areas

* = more for ornamental screens, growth may be poor in strong, windy conditions. Not for cold conditions

| Common name | Botanical name | Details | Code |
|---|---|---|---|
| Abelia | Abelia x grandiflora | glossy, dark green foliage | *T |
| | Aucuba japonica | dense, bushy shrub with glossy dark green foliage | T |
| Box: | | | |
| | Buxus microphylla | slow to grow but long-lived and hardy | |
| | B. sempervirens | glossy leaves, good for screening | |
| | Ceanothus impressus | small, crinkled dark green leaves and attractive deep blue flower clusters | *T |
| Camellia: | | | |
| | Camellia japonica | forms dense neat hedge, but if using different varieties, ensure similar growth habits | * |
| | C. sasanqua | similar to above | T |
| | Cotinus coggygria 'Notcutt's Variety' | deep reddish-purple foliage | |
| | Cotoneaster lacteus | clusters of red fruits in autumn-winter | |
| Euonymus: | | | |
| | Euonymus japonicus 'Ovatus Aureus' | hardy variegated foliage plant, leaves are broadly edged with golden-yellow | TS |
| | E. fortunei 'Silver Queen' | dense growth of dark green leaves, broadly edged with white | T |
| Firethorn: | | | |
| Orange firethorn | Pyracantha angustifolia | sturdy, thorny growth with dull-green foliage, orange berries | T |
| Scarlet firethorn | Pyracantha coccinea | sturdy, thorny growth with dark, glossy foliage and red berries | T |
| Flowering quince | Chaenomeles species | also called 'Japonica', forms dense, spiney hedge | |
| | Hibiscus syriacus 'Oiseau Blue' | good for hedging, carries large, lilac-blue flowers | T |
| Honeysuckle | Lonicera nitida | tiny dark foliage, rapid-growing substitute for box for low hedges but less permanent | T |
| Laurel | Prunus lusitanica | suited to tall hedges in cooler areas | T |
| Lavender | Lavandula dentata | quick low hedge within 6–12 months, best in open position in dry climate | |
| Privet | Ligustrum ovalifolium | commonly used for dense hedging, glossy, mid-green leaves | T |
| | L. vulgare | as above | T |
| Rosemary | Rosmarinus officinalis | low hedge for sunny situations | TS |
| Yew | Taxus baccata | slow-growing conifer | T |

With tall hedges especially, it is preferable to taper the sides slightly towards the top. Otherwise, base growth tends to thin out.

Seedlings of other trees or shrubs sometimes progress unnoticed in a hedge until they become too large to pull out. Some of the main offenders are pittosporum, laurel, large- or small-leafed privet and other berry-producing trees, which birds help to scatter. If these seedlings are no more than about 30 cm (12 in) high, it may be possible to pull them out when the soil has been well-soaked after rain. Otherwise, cut them off 12–15 cm (5–6 in) above ground on a horizontal plane (to avoid run-off), then immediately paint the cut with a glyphosate product as directed on the label. Should they be large plants and produce suckers after treatment, then when most of the leaves have matured, strip these off and paint again with the same mixture.

## PLANTING NEW HEDGES

Favoured clipped evergreen hedges are box, yew or some other conifers. Yew is a relatively slow grower compared to other small-leafed plants. Box (*Buxus*) is also considered very slow but some of the slightly larger and rounder Japanese varieties such as *B. microphylla* var. *japonica* or *B. sempervirens* 'Suffructicosa' are ideal for good-quality, lower hedges 1–2 m (3–6 ft) high if you are prepared to wait a year or two longer for them to mature. The smaller and darker-leafed box varieties or plants such as *Lonicera nitida* are usually favoured for edging rather than hedging (although, as far as I know, when an edge becomes a hedge is yet to be defined!)

Plants forming a hedge are planted much closer together than would normally be the case in a garden. Spacing them about one quarter of their mature size ensures a dense effect, but means their roots are in fierce competition, so it is necessary to keep to a regular feeding program throughout the growing season.

## FORMAL HEDGES

In some settings, a well-clipped formal hedge may fit into the landscape beautifully but to keep its well-groomed appearance it needs to be clipped at least twice a year. This may not be a problem with small hedges less than 2 m (6 ft) high, especially with powered hedge clippers, but becomes a mammoth task, perhaps involving gantry-type ladders, when the hedge reaches a great height.

*Camellia sasanqua* makes an amiable, dark, glossy green hedge and is ideal where space or width is limited as its flexible caney branches can be tied in with neighbouring plants. Any surplus forward growth is trimmed off. Unless buds are also removed, you can still enjoy its autumn flowers. *C. japonica,* although more upright and with larger foliage, also makes an attractive hedge.

BELOW: *All the many species of lavender make marvellous edges or hedges and are well-suited to a full sun position.*

# Plants for Screens and Windbreaks

T = suitable for trimming      S = suitable for coastal areas

| Common name | Botanical name | Details | Code |
|---|---|---|---|
| Alder | *Alnus glutinosa* | semi evergreen in temperate areas, roots can cause problems | T |
| Atriplex: | | | |
| | *Atriplex canescens* | N. American variety, very wind-resistant, requires little trimming | S |
| | *A. halimus* | good for coastal site, silvery-grey foliage | S |
| Bamboos: | | | |
| | *Pseudosasa japonica* (syn. *Arundinaria japonica*) | vigorous bamboo, makes an excellent screen even in exposed conditions | S |
| | *Sasa palmata* | fine foliage, good for screening, but not an exposed site | |
| | *Semiarundinaria fastuosa* | as above | |
| Barberry | *Berberis darwinii* | undemanding hedging with profusion of orange flowers and bluish berries | |
| Cypress: | | | |
| Arizona cypress | *Cupressus arizonica* | attractive grey foliage | TS |
| Monterey cypress | *C. macrocarpa* | excellent windbreak for cooler areas | TS |
| Dogwood | *Cornus sanguinea* | good, informal hedge | T |
| Elder | *Sambucus nigra* | capable of growing almost anywhere, produces delightfully fragrant white flowers and fruits | |
| Field maple | *Acer campestre* | attractive foliage, responds well to trimming | T |
| Hawthorn | *Crataegus* species | good for growing in polluted urban areas, exposed sites and coastal gardens; attractive flowers | S |
| Hazel | *Corylus avellana* | deciduous, with twisted shoots, broad leaves, catkins in winter | |
| Holm oak | *Quercus ilex* | when young, leaves are toothed much like holly leaves | T |
| Laurel: | | | |
| Cherry laurel | *Prunus laurocerasus* | glossy green foliage, tolerates shade; fruiting | T |
| Portugal laurel | *P. lusitanica* | tough plant for dry, cold conditions; also fruiting | T |
| Pine: | | | |
| Beach pine | *Pinus contorta* | good for exposed, windy sites | |
| | *P. x Cupressocyparis leylandii* | vigorous conifer, commonly used for hedging | T |
| Mountain spruce | *Picea engelmannii* | bluish-green foliage, good for a poor site | |
| Radiata pine also known as Monterey pine | *Pinus radiata* | quick-growing windbreak | |
| Viburnum | *Viburnum acerifolium* | attractive autumn foliage | |

## OVERCOMING SLOW GROWTH

One way to ultimately enjoy a slow-growing hedge like yew, or others with the moderate pace of camellias, and still gain fairly rapid screening, is to plant a relatively short-lived quick grower parallel with it. On a large scale where space permits, small quick-growing trees are suitable, although they may need cutting out eventually.

To establish a *Camellia sasanqua* hedge, I successfully used *Grevillea* 'Ivanhoe' about 2 m (6 ft) out from the main hedge so as not to inhibit growth. This upright grower can reach 2 m (6 ft) or more in a year.

Most normally long-lived evergreens are suitable for using as naturally growing screens or formal hedges, including *Photinia glabra* 'Rubens', popular in cool and temperate areas for its glossy red new growth. Two hardy hibiscus, *Hibiscus syriacus* 'Oiseau Blue', syn. *H.s.* 'Blue Bird' and *H.s.* 'Diana', also provide colourful flowers in a sunny position.

*Escallonia* species are similarly generous. The glossy, evergreen foliage is lightly aromatic, wafting its scent on a warm summer day or when cut or bruised. A wealth of summer flowers are borne, in varying shades according to the cultivar. *Escallonia* 'Apple Blossom' is a popular choice, with its pink blooms. It will create an excellent evergreen screen and wind break and is suited to coastal situations.

The buff grey leaves, with mottled grey undersides, of *Elaegnus* x *ebbingei* make an interesting change to the perpetual green of hedging plants. It responds well to clipping, but if left unchecked will flower in the autumn with glorious, highly scented, small white flowers.

## Protecting the Garden from Wind

Solid walls and trees with closely packed foliage offer resistance to strong winds which can surge over them causing worse turbulence on the other side.

A wall with some open work, sparsely foliaged trees graded in height and with a mixture of foliage allows wind to pass through with less intensity.

# TO LAWN OR NOT TO LAWN

You will often hear that the lawn is an essential part of a garden. Certainly a good lawn sets off a garden, in much the same way as a good carpet enhances the appearance of a room. However, there are alternatives if mowing is not for you.

You may well have good reason to prefer polished timber or slate floors in your room, just as your choice may be for paving, gravel or other ground covers rather than lawn grass in the garden.

The alternative materials eliminate mowing although solid paving requires sweeping and regular de-mossing if shaded or damp, while gravel or earthen paths call for weed control and raking to maintain a tidy appearance.

Even if you decide on a wild garden with woodchip or earthen paths meandering through it, you will probably still need weed control to prevent weeds from overtaking the garden and paths. Also, bear in mind that many wild plants are comparatively short-lived and those from different areas may be a challenge to establish. However, if you choose local plant varieties to form the backbone of the garden, and realise that some of the others may be difficult, the project becomes interesting and the result more satisfying. There are also many grafted plants now available which can alleviate the problems associated with climatic conditions.

One of the best arguments in favour of plants indigenous to your area is that they save water. Once established, they should survive with the local rainfall pattern.

On the subject of water, a well-prepared and properly managed lawn does not need copious watering to keep it looking healthy. It is a matter of choosing the right grass type and of regular general lawn care as outlined later in this chapter.

There are many advantages to a lawn. Lawn grass makes the best ground cover for children's play areas, outdoor family sporting activities and clothes-drying areas, and it is pleasant to relax on. Lawns look appealing on any scale, whereas large areas of solid paving have a stark appearance unless interspersed with plant growth in pockets or in a group of pots.

RIGHT: *The sight of a vast curving lawn sweeping into the distance is the goal of many dedicated gardeners.*

108

## REJUVENATING AN OLD LAWN

If the existing lawn area is still reasonably identifiable, it may be just a case of mowing over, then giving the grass a chance to regrow before making a definite decision on its worth.

Allow for the fact that some grasses make little or no regrowth during cold winter conditions.

Should the emerging grass seem fairly well distributed in most parts of the lawn, and of the same type, then the inevitable soft or broad leafed weeds can be eliminated by spraying with any of the proprietary lawn weedkillers. On the other hand, if there is a variety of weedy grasses, it may be better to evenly spray the entire area with glyphosate. A kill with this preparation usually takes about two weeks, providing the weeds are in active growth.

Within three weeks the lawn can safely be prepared for replanting.

Note particularly those shaded areas close to trees or large shrubs where the grass did not recover after the initial mowing. In most well-established gardens, there are invariably areas where the lawn gradually thins out or fails as large shrubs or trees create too much shade and root competition. One or two reluctant growth areas like this can spoil the overall appearance considerably, therefore the lawn should be reshaped to exclude these potential trouble areas. Plants suitable for such conditions are listed on p 34.

One exception is where the entire lawn is in shade for more than about half the day or is in dappled shade. Here, the cool-climate grasses such as the various bent or Kentucky blue grasses will grow in all but semi-tropical to tropical areas. The bent grasses grow in shaded spots in temperate districts during summer as well as winter, providing plenty of water is available, but they may be subject to fungus attack during warm moist conditions. In all cases it is best to confine lawn grass to the areas that suit it best.

There are newer strains of fescue such as 'Arid' available, also 'Sun and Shade', which are recommended for hot or cold climates. These are claimed to be more drought-tolerant and disease-resistant and do not make runners, minimising problems like invasions of garden beds and rockeries.

Bare patches may have also developed where the soil has become severely compacted due to foot traffic where people have taken short cuts, around outdoor eating areas or children's play equipment, etc. This problem is dealt with in the chapter on Rectifying Compacted Soil on p 44.

BELOW: *Lawns and edges can be quite informal as long as you are prepared to be careful in trimming the edges. Here, a natural rock outcrop has been enhanced by a second boulder which reflects the outline of the shadows of the shrubs.*

'Fairy rings' (a circle of lush growth surrounded by a ring of mushrooms) can be an aesthetic problem. It is not always easy to eradicate the fungus. In a top quality lawn the answer may be to remove the turf to a radius of 30 cm (12 in), treat the area with a two per cent formalin solution and then reseed after a month.

## PLANNING THE LAWN SHAPE

The first aim is to exclude the too-shaded or root-infested areas already mentioned, where lawn grass will not grow happily and at the same time achieve a pleasing shape. Plan the shape of your new lawn by laying down a garden hose or flexible rope to define the boundary between lawn grass and garden beds. If you prefer an informal free-flowing rather than angular shape, choose generously sweeping curves. Numerous small curves tend to create a fussy effect and make mowing difficult. Also for the latter reason, where possible, incorporate trees or other major plantings within the garden rather than lawn area. Having said that, however, the appearance of lawn flowing evenly around the trunk of a tree can look superb, providing the grass beyond mower reach is not allowed to rise in an untidy collar around the base of the tree. Avoid this by keeping an 10 cm (4 in)-wide gap that the mower can partly ride over, free of grass around the tree base. From all but a few metres (feet) away, this gives the impression of grass ending neatly at the trunk and avoids the tree trunk being damaged by the mower.

## RENEWING LAWNS

As the soil where the lawn is to be renewed has no doubt become compacted over the years, the newly started grass will make much better root growth and the lawn be more even in quality, if you begin lawn preparation from scratch.

When the soil is just damp and has lost any stickiness, dig it over or have it rotary-hoed to a depth of 10–12 cm (4–5 in). This is also a good time to mix a complete fertiliser or lawn starter into the soil. It may sound confusing but do not use a 'lawn food', as most of these are designed mainly to replace nitrogen taken off by grass clippings, and do not contain enough phosphorus to encourage good germination of seed or strong healthy root growth.

If the soil is known to be acid (as a rough guide, where untreated hydrangeas are normally blue) it will also help if about half a cup per square metre (3-feet square) of garden lime is mixed in with the fertiliser.

The next step is to crumble and settle the roughly dug soil. If rotary-hoed, or dug in the just damp condition as suggested, it can be sufficiently broken up.

The best way of producing a good even lawn that does not later settle into hollows, is to have a good firm but not too compacted base with about 3 cm (1 in) of crumbly soil on top. Levelling is not usually necessary in a lawn renewal project except for bowls, croquet and to some extent for garden furniture placement. It is desirable, however, to have an evenly graded surface. An effective grader can be improvised by using a heavy, timber plank or an old timber window frame with a rope attached to screws near either end. Have the point of attachment about a third of the way in from the front edge. If too close to the front of your improvised grader, it tends to skim over the surface rather than grade off mounds and redistribute the soil where needed. If too far back, the front digs in too much.

After the initial grading, a roller is sometimes used to complete settling of the soil but an equally effective (and much easier!) method is just to systematically walk over it, (providing it is still no wetter than just damp). If you can enlist the aid of family and friends, so much the better! Follow with a final grading. Consider the site well-prepared when walking over any part leaves only light footprints, not sunken treads more than about 1 cm (½ in) deep.

It is worth being particularly fussy in this process, as once turfed it will be very difficult to reshape the soil. Unevenly graded turf can be both jarring and awkward to mow, as the cutter will buck and jolt.

## TURF — THE INSTANT LAWN

Well-laid turf obviously gives instant coverage of the soil and usually looks attractive initially, but needs a week or two to form anchoring and sustaining roots before walking on or mowing the lawn. Naturally, the cash outlay is far greater than for seed.

Professional turf growers now supply machine-cut lawn grass in rolls about 40 cm (16 in) wide, like carpet, which are very easy to lay. Most types of grass are available. Be sure the site is prepared before ordering as these rolls should be laid as soon as possible after delivery.

ABOVE: *The visual appeal of this seat set back from the lawn certainly adds another dimension to this corner of a well-proportioned garden and in this position doesn't inhibit mowing.*

## GREEN ALTERNATIVES TO GRASS

If a certain area of lawn will not be subjected to frequent utility, or is an awkward stretch to mow, alternatives to grass might be considered.

The classic and romantic choice is that of a chamomile lawn. *Anthemis nobilis* has been used for centuries as a fragrant alternative to grass as it will stand up to a certain amount of traffic and does not require mowing. However, if your soil is not well drained and lies wet in the winter it is unlikely to thrive.

Moss is a second attractive alternative, providing you have moist, acidic soil. It looks particularly good as a substitute to grass beneath trees. It is difficult to buy moss from a nursery and so often the best way to establish an area is to encourage the native mosses already growing in your garden. Regularly cleaning off the fallen leaves and giving it space to expand will certainly help. Alternatively, try transplanting clumps in the early spring.

Creeping thyme (*Thymus serpyllum*) is a third possibility and produces a delightful aroma as well as delicate colouring. I have discussed the use of this plant further in the chapter on Ground Covers on p. 88.

## LAWNS FROM SEED

The most economical way to start a lawn, and very satisfactory if sown at the correct time and with the area prepared as indicated previously, is from seed. It is rewarding to see the green fuzz creeping over the soil then intensifying daily. However, it calls for a little more attention to watering during the first few weeks following seed sowing.

Prepare the site as indicated under Renewing Lawns on p 110, noting particularly the reference to fertiliser. The seed may be sown as soon as the surface is raked, even after treading the soil over to consolidate it, but most people prefer to water then leave it stand for a couple of weeks, which then allows the inevitable weed seeds in the soil to germinate. These are easily killed by lightly raking the surface to break the dry soil crust, on a dry sunny day.

As the soil must be kept damp until the young grass seedlings are established, it is advisable to sow, at one time, only the area that a fixed hose sprinkler can cover. This avoids disturbing the surface and damaging emerging seedlings by walking over it to move hoses.

Choose a still day for sowing when the soil surface is dry and crumbly. There are hand-held combined seed sowers and lawn fertiliser plastic broadcaster buckets available in hardware stores and nurseries to give even distribution of grass seeds. It can also be done by hand providing you don't try to broadcast it too far, which usually results in it falling unevenly in a zig-zag pattern.

I prefer to work in strips only about 2 m (6 ft) wide. These can be marked roughly but fairly accurately with such as the back of a rake

BELOW: *When a garden becomes too shady for a lawn to grow well, the lush, verdant growth of ferns can lighten up an area with their bright green fronds. Here, a birdbath complements the growth habit of the two ferns and gives added emphasis to this composition.*

held nearly to its full length to one side while working across the lawn an appropriate distance from the mark on your opposite side.

This way it is easy to keep to the recommended sowing rate for the particular grass. For example, if it is at the rate of 24–30 g per square metre (¾–1 oz per 3 feet square) (which is about a tablespoon or handful), distribute the required amount within the 2 m (6 ft) strip each time you step back 1 m (3 ft).

Another less accurate but popular method of hand-sowing is to halve the seed, broadcast one half up and down the lawn and the other across. The latter spreading rate can then, if necessary, be adjusted.

Provided the soil surface is fairly dry and crumbly, rake it over in a light back and forth motion to cover the seed. Watch carefully and notice that as you rake, the lawn seed finds its way down and disappears into the little furrows made by the tines of the rake.

If the soil is too coarse or damp to respond as suggested, a light scattering of still-fibrous garden or mushroom compost is ideal to anchor the seed against displacement or being washed into drifts by heavy rain or too vigorous watering. It also helps to keep the surface moist.

## WATERING

In the absence of rain, daily watering is advisable to maintain surface moisture. Watering can be tapered off about a week after germination. Use a gentle sprinkler that does not puddle the surface but, when left on long enough, will wet well down into the soil. Once established, condition the grass to dryness by allowing the soil to dry out to the depth of 2–3 cm (1 in).

## MOWING

Let new grass reach about finger length before mowing, then set the mower high enough to remove only about 1 cm (½ in) of the top. Continue this high mowing for the next two weeks, then gradually set the mower a little lower but not to the close shaving stage. Like any other plant, grass develops growth-sustaining nutrients through the action of sunlight on its foliage. Therefore, continuous mowing weakens both top and root growth.

Thinning the growth by cutting grass too low invites weed growth to compete with the grass. Also for the same reason, it is advisable to set the mower a little higher in late autumn when the approaching low temperatures or a sudden cold spell will halt replacement growth of the grass within a few days.

## MOWER STRIPS

Save labour by deterring naturally running grasses from invading garden beds by installing some form of mower strip. They rarely look better than the conventional V-shaped division between garden soil and neatly clipped lawn but are far less labour intensive.

For readers unfamiliar with a mower strip, it consists of either a 12–15 cm (5–6 in) wide strip of concrete, brick or other solid material. In some cases, a paved path may act as a mower strip. To be practical, the mower strip must be flush with the lawn to allow one side of the lawn mower to ride over it. Have the lawn edge even so that a mechanical or manual wheel or crescent-type edger can effectively trim back grass runners.

It is important not to install mower strips prior to starting the lawn, or before it has had a month or so to settle down. Too often they end up above the level of the grass and so become a hindrance rather than an aid to maintenance.

When the soil has settled, it is usually possible to easily spade out a mould for concrete strips, using 10–12 cm (4–5 in)-wide off-cuts of moistened flexible fibreboard as a mould for the sides. A few pegs driven in on the outside will help to hold it more firmly in the shape wanted, and if the tops of each side are kept level, to evenly float the concrete surface.

# *projects*

## TO COMPLEMENT

## THE GARDEN

# RESTORING PATHS AND PAVING

Paths and paved areas are dominant features within a garden. They need to be both practical, providing an even, non-slip surface, while being visually appealing. Restoring them is a satisfying task.

RIGHT: *When restoring an older garden with outdoor areas paved with flagstones, it may only be necessary to reset an occasional loose stone within a step or clear away encroaching overgrowth to restore the paving. Don't be tempted to clear away all the pocket planting and take away the patina it has gained over the years, otherwise much of its charming atmosphere could well be lost.*

OPPOSITE: *Mossy brick paving can be easily cleaned to provide a non-slip surface.*

Overhanging trees, poor drainage or just winter shade can cause havoc with garden paths and paving. These can detract from the welcoming atmosphere that a well-kept pathway imparts to both house and garden.

Paths that are mossy or slippery with green or black algae or moss-type growth can be cleaned with steam or a high-pressure jet of water from portable compressor-type units, available for hire in most areas for the do-it-yourself gardener. Professional path or roof cleaners also offer this service.

Moss or other growth can be cleaned to leave paths looking like new, by watering to evenly wet the growth with a strong solution of

bleach, or by sprinkling swimming-pool chlorine when the path is wet, then brushing in with a firm broom. The bleach or chlorine treatment is more effective during a cool dull day — in hot sunshine, the chlorine gas is expelled too quickly. By wearing a mask, you will avoid inhaling a quantity of this gas. As splashes and run-off may damage surrounding grass and other plants, it is advisable before beginning to move any pot plants and cover susceptible border plants with sheets of newspaper, and after cleaning, to hose liberally to dilute the chlorine.

In older gardens with flagging, especially in damp situations, the cement between the flags may be crumbling. In this state, weeds are likely to be growing through it and the flagstones can be extremely mossy and slippery. It may be necessary to scrape away the bulk of the moss or algae-type growth before cleaning, as suggested for paths.

If persistent weeds with underground runners are present, treat with a fairly strong solution of glyphosate preparation, then after about ten days, clean stonework or pavers as already suggested for paths.

Where most of the path or paved area is affected, and especially if the paving is uneven and laid on the soil rather than sand, it would be as well to lift and relay them. Use a chisel to

# Dividing the Garden

**1.** A complete garden makeover incorporates this interesting feature that divides two level areas. To the right of the long garden is a paved outdoor sitting area while the steps lead to a parterre garden, illustrated on p 6. Parallel rendered brick walls, built 30 cm (12 in)apart, incorporate a two-metre (6 ft)-long pond. Note how the left wall is built up to retain the higher level and to feature the pond.

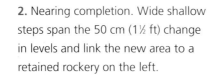

**2.** Nearing completion. Wide shallow steps span the 50 cm (1½ ft) change in levels and link the new area to a retained rockery on the left.

**3.** One year on. A lattice dividing fence positioned behind the wall has been painted to blend with the house trim and is the ideal place for favourite roses, 'Silver Moon', 'Lamarque' and 'Félicité et Perpétué'. The wall behind the pond has been fitted with a Moroccan tile with spout to enhance the water feature and the troughs on either side are planted with *Hebe pimeleoides*.

clean away crumbly cement. Regrade the soil surface if necessary to improve run-off from the area, then spread and grade at least a 3 cm (1 in) deep layer of dry sand.

Position the flags on the sand, either shuffling thicker ones a little deeper or building up more sand under shallower ones, so that the edges of each one follow the same grade. Check this with a straight piece of timber laid on edge above them in both directions. It will see-saw on a high spot or show a gap below it where a spot needs building up.

Leave a space of at least 2 cm (¾ in) between the stones to take the cement. If the paving is rectangular and even spacing is preferred, use a board the required thickness, wedging it between the pavers as you place them.

Random or 'crazy' paving tends to look more interesting, with pavers of variable shapes and sizes and spaces of variable widths between them. Rather than becoming frustrated about not finding a flag to fit evenly, bed a drift of small stones or even river pebbles into the wide gap left when using a smaller substitute. These 'pebbles' can be bedded in when pouring the cement. Rub clean with, say, dry hessian to display them when cement is almost dry. As with more formal cut stone, it is advisable to have at least 1 cm (½ in) gap between the pavers.

Paving material that needs to be cut or trimmed to size should be placed on a bed of sand, the proposed cutting line scratched on the surface using a chisel and straight-edged board as a guide, then with a stone hammer and bolster held upright, tap firmly along this line. Where accurate cutting is needed, this should be done on both sides of the paver.

The stones and sand between pavers should be wet thoroughly before pouring cement into the cracks. Scoop or hose out any sand that has built up more than about one quarter of the depth of the stone.

If only a small area is to be re-worked, a bag of pre-mixed sand-cement can be purchased at

hardware stores, or a mixture can be made up using two or three parts of sand to one of cement. Mix with enough water to allow it to just pour and fill between the pavers when tamped by the edge of the trowel, but not too liquid. It may need re-mixing during use to avoid watery liquid forming on the surface.

## CRACKED OR BROKEN CONCRETE PATHS AND PAVING

One economical and effective replacement for weathered concrete paths where sections of the surface are lifting due to root problems or sinking, is to break all large intact parts into irregular paving-sized pieces. If the concrete pieces are only 6–8 cm (2–3 in) thick, you may find that fairly large areas can be levered up with a crowbar. When these sections are too heavy or

cumbersome to handle, their size can be reduced by raising one side on to a straight piece of timber then hitting about centre with a sledgehammer, buffered by a piece of hardwood across the top of the slab approximately where you want it to crack.

Further division can be carried out this way, or with more accuracy by placing the concrete slab on an even bed of sand then tapping firmly with a stone hammer and bolster along the line where the cut is wanted.

Lay the concrete pieces on a bed of sand as suggested for crazy paving, then cement between them in the same way. The cement can be evened over and any spills removed by rubbing over with dry hessian or similar coarse material when the cement has nearly set, probably the following morning.

ABOVE: *New paving squares replace a broken path within a previously grassed area. Gaps between pavers have been filled with fine gravel which in turn is host to thyme plants. Plants spilling onto the pavers from the surrounding gardens also help to enhance this pleasant outdoor area.*

# RENEWING AND RECYCLING ROCKERIES

*F*ashions change in horticulture just as they do in haute couture, and yesteryear's rockery is no exception. However, don't discard the stones as they are easily recycled.

Many gardens from the late 1950s to the 1970s were landscaped with rockeries. Rock gardens are fine if you enjoy growing rockery plants and can maintain them. Unfortunately, most of the rockeries were called 'easy care' gardens. Soil mounds covered with black plastic sheeting hidden between the stones by woodchip, pine bark or pebbles had plants placed through buttonhole-like cuts in the plastic. The trouble began once tenacious perennial weeds found their way through the rocks and below the plastic sheeting. This also became a haven for ant nests, slugs and other insects.

Here are some suggestions if you find yourself with one of these features.

When growth of invading weeds is active, spray with glyphosate. If the rockery is overcrowded with weeds, it may be easier if any wanted plants are removed and later replaced, or they can be temporarily covered while weeds are sprayed. A few weeks later when all growth appears dead, give a thorough watering to bring any dormant roots into growth. If this does happen, give another few weeks for the regrowth to gain some maturity then give another spraying.

Rake out any remaining plastic sheeting, then if you do not want to indulge in a variety of rockery plants, about three weeks after the last spraying, choose an adaptable and robust cover plant such as fleabane (*Erigeron*) or seaside daisy, star campanula, or any of the other plants suggested for Ground Covers on p 88. The first mentioned especially will rapidly make a dense cover of self-layering stems. For extensive slopes, areas of different carpeting plants plus dense low branching shrubs would look more interesting.

The freestanding rockery may also be stripped of its stone and the soil regraded to form a grassed mound if it would enhance the site. Otherwise, the rocks may be used as a retaining border and the soil to fill a hobby garden in some other part of the garden. Not that a hobby garden needs to be elevated but it does make weeding, planting and so on much more comfortable and easier on your back if you can sit on the retaining wall coping instead of bending while tending the garden.

An elevated garden also provides excellent drainage, especially on clay soil where a grouping of plants, such as Mediterranean herbs, which need perfect drainage, can be grown successfully. The added advantage being that it makes the herbs easy to pick.

*OPPOSITE: A low wall of sandstone pieces is planted behind with sun-loving rosemary 'Blue Lagoon' and lavender, both very appreciative of the perfect drainage afforded by the raised beds.*

For the typical rockery bank where there is a change of level between lawns, if it is no more than a metre or so (around 3 ft) in height, remove the rocks and bevel down the top of the slope until it is gradual enough to mow comfortably. In other words, the top half of the bank is cut off and spread at its base.

If the rocks are not decorative, they may be used as filling by first moving them to the base of the bank then covering with soil. The higher the bank the wider the levelled area must be to achieve comfortable mowing, otherwise the slope can be planted with ground covers.

Incidentally, from the foregoing remarks, it may appear that the author is a rock hater. Quite the contrary! My steeply sloping garden is about 40 per cent rock from the site, mostly moved to retain, and if possible placed to look as if it occurred naturally in its present position. The point I'm trying to emphasise is that rocks are not essential to good landscaping and unless you are fortunate enough to have some on-site or wish to purchase them, they should remain in their natural settings.

When arranging rocks, try to look for and follow the rock strata. This will be more obvious in some rocks than others. Roughly align the strata and the effect will be pleasingly natural.

## RETAINING AND DRY PACK WALLS

A wall built to define a change in level can become a feature itself. Where retaining walls are needed or preferred for changes of level, brick, treated pine logs, railway sleepers, dry pack stone walls, or some form of pre-fabricated concrete are at least as practical as rockeries, usually cheaper and, combined with well-chosen plant growth, can be just as attractive. So often we see a slope retained by expensive, beautifully weathered stone, but where trailing plants have been allowed to take over, any roughly quarried stone or rubble might have been used.

A near-perpendicular dry pack stone wall can be an interesting and effective way to retain

*BELOW: Gentle slope is maintained as wall is built, with base rocks set below ground level and the occasional long rock locking wall into soil behind. Plants can be introduced as wall progresses and a narrow garden bed at the top acts as a buffer between running lawn grasses and rocks.*

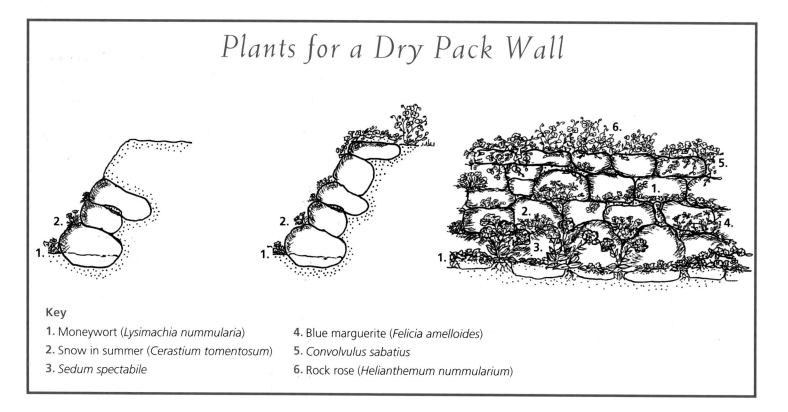

# Plants for a Dry Pack Wall

**Key**

**1.** Moneywort (*Lysimachia nummularia*)

**2.** Snow in summer (*Cerastium tomentosum*)

**3.** *Sedum spectabile*

**4.** Blue marguerite (*Felicia amelloides*)

**5.** *Convolvulus sabatius*

**6.** Rock rose (*Helianthemum nummularium*)

a bank too steep to bevel or grade down with a lawn. It can be made with relatively cheap irregular roughly quarried stone. Its stability depends to some extent on the way the stones are packed with earth, its own weight and particularly on having the wall lying slightly against the bank instead of perpendicular.

Unlike the more formal walls of rectangular cemented stone or pre-cast concrete, the dry pack wall does not need special foundations and drainage provisions. Water causing pressure and swelling soil that can otherwise dislodge a solid wall is eliminated through the spaces between the stones. Trailing plants can be set into soil between stones of the dry pack wall to enhance and increase bonding with the soil.

There is one proviso to the latter, especially if the wall is to be planted. Keep at least a narrow garden bed or path at the top so that running grasses do not creep down and become established amongst the stones. Certainly these grasses can easily be sprayed out with glyphosate preparations but this becomes a difficult task when they are entangled with decorative wanted plants.

## BUILDING A DRY PACK WALL

Start building the dry pack wall by bevelling down the bank to a slope of about 80 degrees. Do this by spading down at approximately this angle from a line say 25 cm (10 in) in behind the top of the bank (providing it is perpendicular and also on its height). Save this soil for filling between and behind the stones.

Make a shallow trench 20–25 cm (8–10 in) out from the base of the bevelled bank to take some of the larger stones. Place these sloping back slightly, each with the flattest side out. Then fill with soil to the top of the stones, firming well behind and between the stones.

The ideal soil is a slightly damp sandy loam that will flow into crevices but not sandy enough to run out between the stones when dry. The second course of stones is then laid so that it sits comfortably on the soil-packed first

ABOVE LEFT: *Two favourite plants which seemingly are always flowering, the blue Alyssum,* Convolvulus sabatius, *and sweet Alice,* Lobularia maritima, *make ideal wall-top subjects.*

ABOVE: *Topping a low wall with wide flags provides both a seat in the sun and a firm footing when tending the garden behind.*

# Trailing Plants for Dry Pack Walls

LS = Light shade is preferable except in cool districts

| Common name | Botanical name | Details | Code |
|---|---|---|---|
| | Aethionema grandiflorum | a short-lived perennial with pink flowers | |
| Ajuga | Ajuga reptans | many cultivars, all with deep-blue flower spikes in early spring | LS |
| | Arenaria balearica | tiny bright-green leaves with scattering of small white flowers in spring | LS |
| | Aubrieta 'Cobalt Violet' | for cool temperate sites | LS |
| Bellflower | Campanula portenschlagiana and C. poscharskyana | both with blue-purple bell flowers on upright stems in spring | LS |
| | Bergenia cordifolia | easy-care plant with large, waxy leaves | |
| Blue marguerite | Felicia amelloides | sky-blue daisy-like flower with yellow centres | |
| Catmint | Nepeta x faassenii | grey-green foliage with lavender-blue flowers | |
| | Convolvulus sabatius | flat, rounded mauve-blue flowers throughout summer | |
| | Cyanthus microphyllus | funnel-shaped, violet-blue flowers | LS |
| | Lewisia 'George Henley' | dense sprays of deep pink flowers; ideal for rock crevices | LS |
| Lithordora | Lithordora diffusa | sprawling sub-shrub for lime-free cool areas | LS |
| Moneywort | Lysimachia nummularia | makes good coverage in moist conditions | |
| Mother of thousands | Saxifraga stolonifera | interesting variegation to foliage | LS |
| Phlox | Phlox subulata | best in cooler areas | |
| Rock rose | Helianthemum nummularium | needs full sun for flowers to open | |
| Rocky Mountain juniper | Juniperus scopulorum 'Repens' | blue-green foliage, will spread up to 1.5 m (4–5 ft) | |
| Rosemary | Rosmarinus officinalis 'Prostratus' | low-growing form of rosemary | |
| | Saxifraga 'Tumbling Waters' | slow-growing; arching sprays of white flowers | |
| | Saxifraga x geum | loose panicles of star-shaped, pink-spotted, white flowers | LS |
| Sedum | Sedum species | various species all with interesting leaf colouring/shapes | |
| Snow-in-summer | Cerastium tomentosum | grey-green foliage with white summer flowers | |
| Swan River daisy | Brachyscome iberidifolia | annual with mauve-blue daisy flowers | |
| Sweet alyssum | Lobularia maritima | both white and mauve tones; self-seeds | |
| Trailing azalea | Loiseleuria procumbens | rose-pink to white flowers in early summer | |
| | Thymus herba-barona | caraway-scented leaves; small lilac flowers in summer | |

course. Place them with the most even side forward and preferably lapping over the joins between the lower stones. Fill any large gaps between them with smaller stones. Variations in height of neighbouring stones add interest and is compensated as you progress. The more important points are that the stones lock in well and that the slight slope towards the bank is maintained as far as possible.

For large walls it is worth taking two straight pieces of timber about the height of the wall, fastening them together at one end and to a short piece at the other so that when the slightly sloping side is held against the wall the other is perpendicular. The latter is easily checked with an upright level or plumb-line (in other words using a piece of string with a small weight at one end held close to the wall to check that it is perpendicular).

An occasional long stone that goes right back to the bank or even cut into it will help lock the wall into the soil behind it. If preferred for extra stability, the top course of stones may be cemented together, or better still, topped with a coping of flat stones.

Plants such as Moneywort (*Lysimachia nummularia*) can be introduced into soil pockets between the stones as the wall progresses. Water sufficiently at this stage to settle them in but avoid making the soil soggy.

If the completed wall looks attractive, it is a pity to cover more than about a third with plants. There are some quite attractive trailers capable of completely covering in relatively short time. Others are much gentler. The growth habits and preference for growing conditions of both are indicated in the list on the opposite page.

LEFT: *A gentle slope has been retained at its base and scattered with large rocks to give the impression of natural outcrops. The 'river' is created by mass planting* Lithodora diffusa *at an angle across the slope.*

# Index

## A

*Abelia grandiflora* 12, 64, 104
*Abutilon megapotamicum* 34, 62
Acacia *see* Wattle
*Acer palmatum* 62
*Achillea nana* 25
*Actinidia kolomikta* 98
*Agapanthus* 32, 38
   *praecox* subsp. *orientalis* 95
*Aethionema grandiflorum* 124
*Ajuga reptans* 92, 100, 124
Alder (*Alnus glutinosa*) 106
Alyssum (*Convolvulus sabatius*) 92, 122, *123*, 124
*Amelanchier* 65
Apple trees 78-81
*Arenaria*
   *balearica* 124
   *montana* 92
Asarabacca (*Asarum europauem*) 88
Aster 82
   Stokes's (*Stokesia laevis*) 87
*Atriplex canescens* 106
*Atriplex halimus* 106
*Aubretia* 'Cobalt Violet' 124
*Aucuba japonica* 24, 34, 104
Azalea 12, 16, 43, 62, 65, **70–73**

## B

Baby's tears (*Soleirolia soleirolii*) 88
Bamboo
   *Pseudosasa japonica* 106
   *Sasa palmata* 106
   *Semiarundinaria fastuosa* 106
Barren's Wort (*Epimedium rubrum*) 88
Bellflower
   *Campanula poscharskyana* 90, 120, 124
   *C. potenschlagiana* 90, 120, 124
*Berberis*
   *darwinii* 62, 106
   *thunbergii* 24
*Bergenia cordifolia* 92, 124
Bittersweet (*Celastrus scandens*) 98
Box elder (*Acer negundo* 'Variegatum') 24
*Brachyglottyis greyi* 26
*Brachyglottyis monroi* 62
Broom (*Cytisus* x *praecox*) 24
Bugle (*Ajuga reptans*) 92, 100, 124
Busy Lizzy (*Impatiens walleriana*) 92

Butterfly bush
   *Buddleia davidii* 64, 84
   *B. alternifolia* 64
   *B. globosa* 64
   *B. salvifolia* 26
Box
   *Buxus microphylla* var. *japonica* 62, 104, 105
   *Buxus sempervirens* 'Suffruticosa' 20, 104, 105

## C

*Camellia* 12, 20, 34, 65, **66–69**
   *japonica* 34, 66, 68, 104, 105
   *nitidissima* 66
   *sasanqua* 31, 34, 66, 68, 69, 84, 104, 105, 107
   x *williamsii* 'Waterlily' 20
Cardoon (*Cynara cardunculus*) 25
Catmint (*Nepeta* x *faassenii*) 25, 124
Ceanothus 24, 53, 62
   'Blue Pacific' 36
   *impressus* 104
   *papillosus* 62
Cedar
   Atlantic 41
   Atlas (*Cedrus atlantica*) 26, 53
   *Cedrus deodara* 53
   *Cedrus libani* 53
*Chaenomeles* 65
Chamomile 88
   *Anthemis nobilis* 112
   *Chamaemelum nobile* 92
Cherry
   flowering (*Prunus serrulata* 'Kanzan') 36, 60
   Japanese (*Prunus serrulata*) 54
   Taiwan (*Prunus campanulata*) 54
*Chimonanthus* 65
Chinese elm (*Ulmus parvifolia*) 36
*Choisya ternata* 62
Cigar plant (*Cuphea ignea*) 62
*Clematis*, 31
   *armandii* 94, 98
   'Jackmanii' 98
   *macropetala* 98
   *montana* 98, 100
   'Nelly Moser' *42*, 98
   'Perle d'Azur' 99
   'Star of India' 98
conifers 22, 24, 26, *47*, 55, 59, 105

*Convolvulus sabatius* 92, 122, *123*, 124
*Corylopsis pauciflora* 62
Cosmos 87
*Cotinus* species 62, 104
*Cotoneaster* 12, 55
   *frigidus* 55
   *horizontalis* 62
   *lacteus* 104
   *serotinus* 55
Cotton lavender (*Santolina chamaecyparissus*) 24, 25
Crab-apple *56*, 60
   *Malus floribunda* 20, 54
   *Malus* x *purpurea* 54
Crape myrtle (*Lagerstroemia indica*) 17, 54, 58, 63
Creeper
   Chinese trumpet (*Campsis grandiflora*) 99
   Flame (*Tropaeolum speciosum*) 98
   Trumpet (*Campsis radicans*) 98
   Virginia (*Parthenocissus quinquefolia*) 99
Creeping Phlox (*Phlox stolonifera*) 92
*Cyanthus microphyllus* 124
Cypress
   Arizona (*Cupressus arizonica*) 26, 106
   *Cupressus sempervirens* 'Swane's Golden' 20
   Monterey (*Cupressus macrocarpa*) *23*, 106

## D

Daisy
   African (*Arctotis hybrida*) 25
   Aurora (*Arctotis* hybrids) 24, 38, *56*, 91
   blue kingfisher 82
   creeping (*Wedelia trilobata*) 90
   Easter 87
   Margeurite *56*, 82, 94
   blue (*Felicia amelloides*) 122, 124
   seaside (*Erigeron karvinskianus*) 93, 120
   shasta 87
   Swan River (*Brachycome multifida*) 86, 93, 124
Daphne 43, *56*, 65
design plans
   creating vistas *20–21*
   dividing with style *100*, *118*
   makeover for a mature garden 36–37
   outdoor living *17*
   plants for a dry pack wall *122*

protecting the garden from wind *107*
shrub and perennial border *84–85*
taming an unkempt garden *31*
*Dierama pulcherrimum* 95
Dog's fennel (*Anthemis tinctoria*) 92
Dogwood
   *Cornus florida* 20
   *C. sanguinea* 106
Dusty miller (*Senecio cineraria*) 24, 25, 65

## E

*Elaeagnus pungens* 'Maculata' 34, 62
*Elaeagnus* x *ebbingei* 107
Elder (*Sambucus nigra*) 106
Elm
   Chinese (*Ulmus parvifolia*) 36
   golden (*Ulmus procera*) 54
   Japanese (*Zelkova serrata*) 54
*Erica* 43
   *canaliculata* 62
*Eryngium variifolium* 25
*Escallonia macrantha*
   'Apple Blossom' 17, 84, 107
   'Rosea' 84
Eucalypts *15*, 24, 26, 55, 56
*Euonymus fortunei* 62, 104
*Euonymus japonicus* 104
*Euphorbia amygloides* var. *robbiae* 32
*Euphorbia griffithii* 100

## F

*Fatsia japonica* 16, 34
*Felicia amelloides* 124
Fern
   fishbone (*Nephrolepis*) 90
   heart's tongue (*Asplenium scolopendrium*) 90
   maidenhair (*Adiantum* species) 90
   soft shield (*Polystichum setiferum*) 12
   sword (*Nephrolepis cordifolia*) 90
   tree (*Dicksonia antarctica*) 33, 34, 36
Firethorn
   orange (*Pyracantha angustifolia*) 104
   scarlet (*Pyracantha coccinea*) 104
Forget-me-not (*Anchusa capensis*) 87
Foxglove (*Digitalis purpurea*) *35*, 87
Fruit trees 78–81
Fuchsia 34, 63

# PHOTOGRAPHIC CREDITS

Our many thanks to the owners of gardens photographed in this book:

Bruce and Margaret Appleton, East Malvern, Victoria: 119

Herb and Nola Bennetto, Kew, Victoria: 110, 111

Robin and Jane Brett, Canterbury, Victoria: 24, cameo 108, 114

Malcolm and Margaret Campbell, Hawthorn, Victoria: 61

Barry and Jean Cole, Hawthorn East, Victoria: cameo 12

Bob and Lynne Connell, Hawthorn, Victoria: cameo 102

Val Dunn, Glen Iris, Victoria: cameo 82

Richard and June Fullager, Kew, Victoria: cameo 27, 39, 57

Fabrizio and Diana Galimberti, Hawthorn, Victoria: 3, 10 (bottom right), 14 (bottom left), 35, 41 (bottom left), cameo 42, 79, 121

Elisabeth Giddy, Hawthorn, Victoria: 5, 40, 41 (bottom right), cameo 74

The late Mrs Goode, Cantervury, Victoria: cameo 9, cameo 32, 108

Anthea Hill, formerly of Malvern, Victoria: 53, 83

Anna and John Holdsworth, Malvern, Victoria: 33

Alton and Gwen Jackson, Surrey Hills, Victoria: 30 (bottom left and right)

June Jojic, Malvern, Victoria: cameo 18

John and Beverley Joyce, Toorak, Victoria: 109, 112

Lorrie Lawrence, Hawthorn East, Victoria: 11, 13, cameo 38, cameo 116, 117, cameo 14; formerly of Kew, Victoria: 105

Jim and Noreen McCarthy, Kooyong, Victoria: cameo 120, 123 (top left)

Rob and Carolyn Macafee, Hawthorn East, Victoria: 102 (bottom left)

Michael, Maria and Andrew McGarvie, Ivanhoe, Victoria: 45,

John Moran and the late Mary Moran, Toorak, Victoria: 101 (bottom right)

Richard Nelson-Jones. Formerly of North Balwyn, Victoria: 8

Peter Nicholls and Clare Coney, Surrey Hills, Victoria: 63

Keva North, Canberra, ACT: 6 (top left, top right and bottom), 118 (top, middle and bottom)

Bruce and Andrea Pulbrook, Hawthorn East, Victoria: cameo 10

Frank and Janet Pyke, Hawthorn East, Victoria: 28

Allan Seale, 42 (bottom), cameo 47, 49, cameo 60, 65, cameo 66, 69, cameo 70, 72 (top left), 75, 76 (left), 77 (bottom left and right), 90, 95, 101 (bottom left), 125

Nona and Cyril Seward, Kew, Victoria: cameo 14, 15, 50, 67, 87

David and Brenda Skelton, Hawthorn East, Victoria: 59

Reg and Elaine Smith, 'Earimil' in Mt Eliza, Victoria: 1, 2, 23, 73, 97, 103 and cameo 115

In Stephanie's Restaurant garden, Hawthorn East, Victoria: 76 (top right)

Victor Stoller, Woodend, Victoria: cameo 29

Cecily Tulloch, Kew, Victoria: 71

University College, Parkville, Victoria: 96

Jill Williams, Malvern, Victoria: cameo 22, 116

Kathy Wright, Brighton, Victoria: 91

Our thanks also to Tony Hitchin and *New Home Magazine*, the *Herald Sun* and to *Australian Home Beautiful* 1988-96. Also to photographers Gary Chowanetz, Robin Gould, Chris Groenhout, Shannon McGrath and Mark Taylor. Other photographers include Lorrie Lawrence, Keva North and Allan Seale, Shaen Adey/NHIL: cameo 16, Denise Greig/NHIL: page 19, cameo 44, cameo 51, 64, 74 (bottom right), cameo 78, 80 (top and bottom), 81 (top and bottom), 93 (bottom). Thanks to the owners of gardens featured in cameo 30, 76, cameo 88 and 89. Also, thanks to photographer Derek St. Romaine: page 42 (bottom), 78 (bottom) RHS Wisley, 79 and 81 (left) West Dean, Sussex, 99 The Garden of the Rose, and 101 (left) Garden: Mrs Thompson, Sun House, Suffolk.